Male and Female Graduate Students

Lewis C. Solmon

Published in Cooperation
with the Higher Education
Research Institute

The Praeger Special Studies program —
utilizing the most modern and efficient book
production techniques and a selective
worldwide distribution network—makes
available to the academic, government, and
business communities significant, timely
research in U.S. and international economic, social, and political development.

Male and Female Graduate Students

The Question of Equal Opportunity

PRAEGER SPECIAL STUDIES IN U.S. ECONOMIC, SOCIAL, AND POLITICAL ISSUES

Praeger Publishers   New York   Washington   London

Library of Congress Cataloging in Publication Data

Solmon, Lewis C
    Male and female graduate students.

    (Praeger special studies in U.S. economic, social, and
political issues)
    Bibliography: p.
    Includes index.
    1. Graduate students—United States.   I. Title.
LB2371.S64   378.1'553'0973   75-43725
ISBN 0-275-22870-3

PRAEGER PUBLISHERS
111 Fourth Avenue, New York, N.Y. 10003, U.S.A.

Published in the United States of America in 1976
by Praeger Publishers, Inc.

Printed in the United States of America

The research reported herein was performed pursuant
to a grant from the National Institute of Education, U.S.
Department of Health, Education, and Welfare (Project
Number 3-3006). Contractors undertaking such projects
under Government sponsorship are encouraged to express
freely their professional judgment in the conduct of the
project. Points of view or opinions stated do not, therefore, necessarily represent official National Institute
of Education position or policy.

This study of differential opportunities for men and women graduate students was undertaken for four reasons: (1) to help reach a consensus on a proper and operational definition of sex discrimination in graduate schools, (2) to turn the debate over sex discrimination toward efforts to quantitatively document the allegations previously substantiated by anecdotes, (3) to see whether the affirmative action legislation regarding students, which has been imposed on graduate institutions and caused great havoc in their operation, is required or justified; that is, whether differential treatment exists, and if so, whether it is the fault of institutions or of earlier conditioning of both sexes by society, and (4) to cope with the statement by my five-year old daughter, Kira, that she will become a nurse and her boyfriend will become a doctor because girls are always nurses and boys are always doctors.

The analyses presented in this book provide some evidence that differential treatment of men and women graduate students exists, but also some data indicating that things have improved compared with conditions in earlier eras. Some readers will be disturbed that differences in treatment of the sexes still exist. Others may be upset by implications that things are better, since these people believe that evidence of this type takes the wind out of the sails of the women's movement. I believe that leaders of the movement for women's equality should be heartened by data which show their efforts are effective. Moreover, if this study stimulates other researchers to collect more data, to provide better evidence on either the existence, or nonexistence, of differential treatment of men and women graduate students, the efforts described here will have been worthwhile.

The monograph begins with a review of earlier discussions of sex discrimination in the graduate schools. This review is followed by attempts to document and explain differences by sex in the admissions process, time spent in graduate study, geographic and interinstitutional mobility, and financial aid practices. It is in these areas that the most explicit charges of differential treatment of the sexes have been made; these are also areas where new data can be brought to bear on the issues.

This study was conducted over a two-year period with the assistance of many individuals: Kohann Whitney, Karla Kroesing, Paul Hemond, and Susan Cross served as research assistants. Susan Cross was primarily responsible for Chapter 1 which reviews the literature, and for the appendices on catalog content and institutional reports. Beverly T. Watkins made the manuscript readable by editing it in its entirety. Data files were provided by Penny Foster of the National Science Foundation, Clairebeth Cunningham and W.C. Kelly of the National Research Council, Alexander W. Astin of the University of California, Los Angeles, and Robert Altman of the Educational Testing Service. Special thanks are due the graduate deans who assisted in the study by responding to a survey in fall 1973.

Michelle Patterson and Clairebeth Cunningham deserve thanks—and probably blame—for encouraging me to undertake this study and for providing comments on earlier drafts. Michele Harway also provided valuable comments at several stages. C.E. Christian prepared the index and made numerous useful suggestions which improve this study.

As usual, my wife Vicki has been a constant source of encouragement; my daughter Kira has been a strong supporter so that she would see her name appear in another book. Matthew, two years old and completely oblivious of what I was doing, made me work more quickly so I could play with him when I was done.

CONTENTS

LIST OF TABLES

Discrimination against women has been a major theme in higher education over the last decade. Attention has focused on charges of differential treatment of women graduate students and women faculty. A review of the literature indicates the content and bases of the various allegations and the current state of the research into areas of possible discrimination.

Institutional policies and practices that affect prospective and enrolled graduate women include admissions procedures, financial aid, and the maintenance of an environment that some think is inadequate to the needs of women students. The lack of day-care facilities, gynecological services, and part-time study opportunities is seen by some as evidence that certain campuses do not accommodate women as well as they accommodate men. Some think faculty are less accessible to women students and that men students receive more encouragement through working relationships with professors.

Institutional hiring practices affect the career advancement of a woman graduate. Claims have been made that men applicants are favored over women and that promotion and salary schedules are not comparable. Antinepotism policies have been attacked. The underrepresentation of women on the faculty, plus poor treatment, is said to hinder not only the female faculty but also women graduate students, who are not exposed to many successful academic women.

DEFINING DISCRIMINATION OR EQUITY

No current definition of discrimination or equity could gain universal acceptance. Indeed, the confusion of both researchers and policy makers over this concept is great. Current definitions of equity, such as "the state of being just, impartial, and fair" (from a popular dictionary) or the generally accepted "equal opportunity" for each sex, have no operational significance without defining justice, impartiality, fairness, and opportunity. Clearly, what is just or fair or equal opportunity in certain respects is unjust, unfair, or unequal opportunity in others. A measuring rod is necessary to evaluate these terms. Similarly, the frequently mentioned "full participation" is unclear. Does this mean that all men and women in America get a Ph.D.? Certainly not. Should everyone make full use of his or her talents? Probably. But which talents: those possessed at birth or talents acquired through high school? What if the talents of women are not as well developed as those of men?

Defining equity is a particular problem when the concept is interjected at a point in the life cycle when many differences between the sexes already have been established. If equity between the sexes was sought from birth onward, members of each sex would have to be treated identically. However, by the time an individual is seriously considering post-high school or postcollege activities, the treatment of the sexes has already been different. When a high school boy or girl contemplates the future, each has already been exposed to cultural influences ranging from nursery rhymes to television programs that clearly indicate that the accepted paths for men and women diverge. Obviously, equal treatment of men and women beginning with the senior year of high school would result in outcomes different by sex, since young men and women have different knowledge and are regarded differently by society at that point.

A major decision about the definition of equity, therefore, must be whether to accept equal treatment or to require compensatory treatment. Equal treatment means identical amounts of advice and encouragement and identical criteria for decisions on admissions, financial aid, and the like. However, previous inputs into, say, women's thought processes might require differentiated counseling and encouragement. Moreover, different channeling in elementary and secondary school might imply that admissions and aid decisions should be based on different criteria explicitly related to earlier training and to success in reaching goals that have been differentially established by sex. Equal treatment of people with differing experience will result in different opportunities for men and women. Rather than equal treatment for all, equity for members of each sex in all likelihood will require differential treatment by sex.

It is usually argued that equity will be achieved when there is no discrimination and no prejudice. To discriminate is defined in Webster's New Collegiate Dictionary as (1) "To mark or perceive the distinguishing or peculiar features of" and (2) "To make a difference in treatment or favor on a basis other than individual merit." In a world of scarce resources, allocations are generally based on some peculiar features of individuals or groups. This approach would be acceptable if it could be agreed that the perceived differences among individuals did exist and that the characteristics that determined resource distribution were logical and just measures. Problems can arise when rewards are based on characteristics that people feel should not be rewarded, or when people disagree over the particular characteristics of those receiving the rewards.

This latter situation may involve prejudice—literally, "pre-judging." People often base their perceptions of individual traits on past observations of groups of which they were members or on earlier experiences no longer relevant. One reason for disagreement over individual characteristics is that precise information is unobtainable or at least expensive. Those distributing rewards may think the cost of an imperfect, erroneous, or unjust distribution is less than that of ensuring equitable distribution. This is not discrimination solely by prejudice; rewards are simply based on estimates of individual merit that are not exactly correct.

These processes lead to some diverse policy implications. Assume that society views the distribution of a certain commodity (such as admission to postsecondary education) among individuals as inequitable. Does this inequity result from ignorance of the distribution of particular traits among groups, or are decision makers acting invidiously and explicitly making decisions on grounds other than merit? Merit might be defined as including traits that increase probability of graduation (ability, motivation, persistence), although other definitions also are possible. If inequity results from ignorance, one might advocate improving the information system so those making distributions will be aware of the characteristics of particular individuals or groups. However, if those making distributions are using an undesirable criterion, one might advocate legislation to change criteria and to police distribution activities.

Sociologists distinguish between two types of discrimination: that due to decisions by individuals or groups and that due to the organization of institutions (or the rules of the game). In the second type, a group may be discriminated against without any individual taking explicit action; however, rules can be changed by people to prevent ongoing discrimination.

Those who believe that discrimination against women exists in education assume that decisions are based on nonmeritorious criteria and, hence, that legislation is necessary to change those criteria. One underlying assumption is that differences between the sexes relevant to postsecondary education do not exist, and that it is merely the desire of those in power to maintain their positions that leads to second-class status for women. Or perhaps differences exist, but the rules of the game favor men. Differential distribution of rewards from education may be due to ignorance of the characteristics of each sex. However, the current status of the two sexes in education could result, at least in part, from actual differences, perhaps in their desire for a specific level of education, given early experiences.

Individuals concerned with the treatment of women in higher
education have defined discrimination in various ways, but they agree
on several points. Discrimination exists when women are judged on
group performance rather than on individual merit. Educational opportunity should depend not on class stereotypes based on the color or
shape of one's skin (Sandler 1972) but upon individual needs, desires,
and potential for contribution, according to Cross (1972, p. 8).
Freeman (1970) believes that the possibility of being discriminated
against is as debilitating to women as actual acts of injustice:

> To go through life never really knowing shether one is
> seen as an individual or as a category, to engage in one's
> work with questions as to how much of it will be judged
> strictly on its merit and how much as the product of a mem-
> ber of a group, to be unable to say that one is treated the
> same as others without hidden bias—these uncertainties
> in themselves wreak their own havoc regardless of what
> the real situation may be (p. 118).

The question of competency enters most discussions of discrimination: "When a woman with superior qualifications is bypassed in favor
of a man with inferior qualifications, prejudiced discrimination may
legitimately be charged," said Bernard (1964, p. 49). This begs the
question of defining "superior qualifications." Bernard, pointing out
that the best competitors suffer most from prejudiced discrimination,
said, "Less qualified candidates can be rejected on many functional
grounds: they are not well trained, they are not competent, they do
not have the skills, etc. It is only when all other grounds for rejection
are missing that prejudiced discrimination per se is brought into play."
In a definition of discrimination against women professionals that also
applies to academic women, Theodore (1971) said discrimination
"occurs when females of equivalent qualification, experience, and
performance as males do not share equally in the decision-making
process nor receive equal rewards. These rewards consist of money,
promotions, prestige, professional recognition and honors" (p. 27).
Another frequently mentioned concomitant of discrimination
against women involves restrictions or barriers within institutions and
society. Theodore (1971) referred to the "lack of normative patterns to
facilitate normal entry into the professions and the imposition of barriers
which limit access to both the organization and to professional
colleagues." Roby (1973) defined institutional barriers as "the policies
and practices in higher education which hinder women in their efforts
to obtain advanced education. These barriers include practices
pertaining to student admissions, financial aid, student counseling,
student services, and curriculum" (p. 38).
Any "barriers to individual development" constitute discrimination, according to Cross (1974). "To discriminate is to deny freedom

of choice; it is to make decisions affecting the lives of individuals <u>without their consent</u> and frequently without their knowledge." This freedom of choice may be denied "by institutional practices that are consciously or unconsciously discriminatory," "by social pressures that define acceptable behaviors for women," or by women's "own social conditioning and attitudes regarding women's roles" (p. 30).

LOCATING DISCRIMINATION IN HIGHER EDUCATION

That fewer women than men are in graduate school and in faculty positions is well documented (Harris 1970; Roby 1973; Solmon 1973). The proportion of women in higher education decreases as the level of academic attainment advances; approximately equal numbers of men and women enter U.S. colleges and universities as undergraduates, about one-third of the students admitted to graduate school are women, and less than one-fourth of the academic positions in the country are filled by women. What is not so apparent is whether the relatively small number of women in graduate education is the end product of years of discriminatory practices by society, or of explicit policies of institutions of higher education. If discrimination is occurring, where does it exist and to what extent? The major thrust of the literature on discrimination is toward understanding the dynamics of women's exclusion to determine possible causes and to suggest remedies.

Much controversy arises over practices that seem discriminatory to one person but legitimate to another. Bernard (1965), who faced this problem in her studies, thought that "the subject of discrimination on whatever basis—age or race, as well as sex—is extraordinarily complex, subtle, and difficult to be unequivocal about. Discrimination is extremely difficult to demonstrate and evidence—for or against it— is not interpreted the same way by all observers" (p. 175).

Some investigators have concluded that overt discrimination does exist. Frank Newman, who headed a task force investigating higher education for the U.S. Office of Education (1971), reported that "discrimination against women, in contrast to that against minorities, is still overt and socially acceptable within the academic community" (p. 80). Jencks and Riesman (1969) cited the sex quotas of private institutions as a sign of open discrimination since these quotas are established "quite independently of the number or talent of each group of applicants" (p. 294). Roby (1973) quoted Peter Muirhead's discussion of quotas in his testimony before a House subcommittee investigating sex discrimination in higher education in 1970. Muirhead, then associate commissioner of education, referred to "fixed percentages of men and women" admitted each year. "At Cornell University, for example, the ratio of men and women remains 3 to 1 from year to year; at Harvard/Radcliffe it is 4 to 1" (p. 42).

Certain educators in positions where discrimination may be observed first hand, have acknowledged its presence. In comments at Massachusetts Institute of Technology on American women in science and engineering, Bernard (1965) said she was rebuked by both Ben Euwema and Reisman, who read the manuscript of <u>Academic Women</u>, for not uncovering more evidence of discrimination. She noted that "both these men have sat on committees selecting candidates of one kind or another, and they know intimately the processes involved. They have heard the criteria discussed, including the sex of the applicant. If <u>they</u> say there is discrimination against women in academia, it must surely be there. But it is very difficult to prove" (p. 177). It is difficult to prove because it is difficult to define.

Alan Pifer (1971), president of the Carnegie Corporation, related his perception of discrimination in a speech to the Southern Association of Colleges and Schools. "That there <u>is</u> discrimination against women in higher education cannot be denied. Some of you in this room, along with men elsewhere, have practiced it, however unconscious you may have been of doing so. But to ascribe the situation entirely to prejudice against women is simply ludicrous. It is a far more complicated matter than that" (pp. 5-6).

Lewis (1969) suggested that discrimination, if it does exist, may be justifiable. "In actuality, it can be argued that graduate admissions committees should be more discriminatory than they are now, if 'discrimination' is interpreted in its basic sense of making careful and wise decisions regarding the potential outcomes of candidates for admissions" (p. 30). Lewis argued that if one looks at the past performance of young graduate women, one can predict low completion rates.

Intentional discrimination is not considered the major cause of women's minimal participation in higher education. The Carnegie Commission (1973) reported that

> It would have been satisfying to state . . . that a systematic pattern of discrimination is (or is not) leveled against women in graduate and professional school. Our data, however, do not substantiate either the presence or the absence of such discrimination. What has been borne out is that within graduate education there is a great deal of inequality based on sex. But inequality is not the same thing as discrimination (p. 137).

Bernard (1964) suggested that women may choose not to enter graduate school rather than be refused access: "The picture seems to be one not of women seeking positions and being denied, but rather one of women finding alternative investments of the time and emotion more rewarding, one in which academic professions—because of changing role demands, and changing faculty-student relationships, and

changing faculty-administration relationships—seem relatively less
attractive than in the past" (p. 67). Prejudiced discrimination is not
a problem en masse but is most likely to affect isolated cases of top-
flight women scholars.

Like Bernard, most researchers have found it exceedingly difficult to substantiate discrimination with statistics. As Roby (1973)
pointed out,

> Whether and to what extent women are discriminated
> against in college admissions is difficult to determine.
> No national statistics are available on college applicants
> who have been rejected by institutions of higher educa-
> tion. We know the characteristics of those who are accepted
> and we can compare women enrollees with men enrollees,
> but we do not know if the rejection rate is higher among
> women applicants, nor whether this varies by type of
> institution (pp. 38-39).

Our study will provide evidence on this issue. In the absence of this
information, Roby looked at the number of women at each academic
level and proposed that more women would be represented if the
superior academic qualifications of women students were considered.
She said, "we must examine indirect and partial evidence" resolving
the questions of discrimination.

Harris (1970) faced the same difficulty as Roby in trying to
uncover possible discrimination. "That the overall distribution of
women in institutions of higher education is highly suggestive of
discriminatory attitudes and practices no one can deny, but research
into the problem of discrimination against women is handicapped at
present by the scarcity of studies of individual colleges and universities" (p. 283). She believed that certain areas of discrimination
were covert and referred to de facto discrimination (practices that
ignore women's needs). Harris's examples of de facto discrimination
include the lack of serious study of women by academics ("women are
seen from the male perspective"), the lack of childcare facilites,
proper health services for women, and maternity leaves.

Freeman (1972) summarized de facto discrimination: "As long as
the university does not concern itself with the variety of life styles
prevalent among academic women and the many needs they have that
differ from those of men, it will inevitably discriminate against otherwise qualified women" (p. 16). The college environment is unwelcom-
ing to women students and faculty, who are left with the feeling that
they have not gained full acceptance. "If the university and the
behavior of its faculty does not directly discriminate against women,
their benign neglect does the job far more insidiously" (p. 16).

Caplow and McGee (1958) also saw women excluded from the
academic world more from neglect than from rejection. "Women tend

to be discriminated against in the academic profession, not because
they have low prestige but because they are outside the prestige
system entirely and for this reason are of no use to a department in
future recruitment" (p. 111). Campbell (1970) pointed out that
women's absence from higher education is a well-established tradition:
"The attitudes that govern the procedures and structures of American
higher education are not consciously inhumane, of course; they are
'discriminatory by inheritance'" (p. 57).

    The egalitarian ideals of the higher educational system would
appear to denounce discriminatory practices. As summarized by
Caplow and McGee (1958), "the university is committed to the ideal
of advancement by merit. In a community of scholars, scholarly
performance is the only legitimate claim to recognition" (p. 192).
Berelson (1960) also states that "the graduate school, in its dominating
concern with research, admits students primarily or exclusively on
the basis of one criterion: intellectual capability" (p. 57).

    Some, arguing that judgment by merit operates less in selecting
graduate than undergraduate students, thought that women are treated
more equitably as undergraduates than as students attempting to enter
the more rigorous regime of graduate school: "As the competition and
the discrimination become stiffer—from undergraduate student to
graduate student to faculty member—women who persevere become
increasingly aware of discrimination of the part of educational institutions" (Harris 1974, p. 34). The scholars' persistent belief in liberal
education for everyone accounts for acceptance of undergraduate women,
while other nonacademic criteria are partially responsible for selecting
graduate students (Jencks and Riesman 1969, p. 295).

SOCIALIZATION FACTORS

    The attitudes of women toward themselves, as well as the
attitudes of men educators toward women, are factors in women's
underrepresentation in higher education. Hence, it is important to
see how socialization attitudes based on prevailing societal norms
affect both women who might apply to graduate school and those who
are members of the academic community.

    The most frequently cited societal expectation concerns a
woman's role as wife and mother. Cross (1974) illustrated the prevailing attitude toward graduate study for women: "Few would maintain that a master's degree in any field is necessary or even desirable
for women who expect to live out their lives as wives and mothers,
and many people would argue that a Ph.D. is a downright disadvantage"
(p. 38). Assumptions are made that women will drop out of graduate
school to get married and bear children, or that family obligations
will limit their productivity if they do earn degrees:

Many graduate and professional programs for which members of both sexes commonly apply tend to discriminate against women, and many authorities believe they have good reason. Women are poorer bets than men to finish such a program, and those who do are less likely to use their education productively. A university feels some obligation not only to educate individuals, but also to be of benefit to society; thus if an admissions committee must choose between a capable man and a capable woman for a place in its program, the choice can logically be made in favor of the man (Lewis 1968, p. 212).

Bernard (1964) recounted the view of one department head: "I think that when the state and our staff invest large sums of money and a great deal of time and effort in the professional development of a woman, we take a far greater risk than when we make a similar investment in a man. For this reason it seems sensible to me that when we are considering male and female candidates of presumably equal calibre, some small preference should be given to the men" (p. 49).

The faculty attitude "that women won't finish . . . and if they do . . . that they won't be in the national market place as professionals" becomes institutionalized in recruiting, admissions, and funding policies (Fox 1970, p. 34). The result is a vicious circle: because certain policies do disregard women's needs, women fulfill the prophecy by dropping out or taking longer to finish.

Expectations for women's performance are imposed many years before the decision to attend graduate school is made. "It [discrimination] begins in the cradle, where boys and girls begin receiving different messages about their future roles" (Epstein 1970, p. 50). The work of Maccoby (1966) and Kagan and Moss (1962) supported the belief that sex role behavior is learned in early childhood. But, as Roby (1973, p. 44) indicated, "There is no way we can draw up a balance sheet that distinguishes the extent to which discrimination operates to exclude women from advanced graduate and professional training and the extent to which self-exclusion from advanced training results from the sex-role socialization that inhibits women's aspirations."

Roby cited a study of high school students by Sewell and a study of college students by Davis to show that the aspirations of women are lower than those of men. The high school girls in Sewell's study received less encouragement from parents and teachers to "aim high" in their life goals. The college women in the Davis study were less likely than the men to make plans to attend graduate school, even though more were in the top half of the class.

Horner (1970) explained women's thwarted ambition by focusing on socialization processes: women have a "motive to avoid success; i.e., a disposition or tendency to become anxious about 'achieving' because they anticipate or expect negative consequences (i.e., unpopularity or loss of feminity) because of success." This motive is "a latent, stable, personality disposition, acquired early in life in conjunction with sex, sex role standards, and sexual identity" (pp. 16-17). Attitudes of parents and men peers toward appropriate sex role behavior aroused the fear of success in Horner's subjects, apparently lowering their aspirations. Horner's findings support Kamarovsky's argument that many college women sense a change in their parents' attitudes: Values related to marriage and feminine ideals are rewarded more than scholarly study.

Rossi (1965) illustrated the negative feelings of college women toward "inappropriate sex role behavior" in a study of women in medicine, engineering, and the sciences. When college women were asked why so few American women enter these fields, many responded that men disapprove. In engineering, the three reasons given most frequently were: "Women are afraid they will be considered unfeminine if they enter this field"; "Most parents discourage their daughters from training for such a field"; and "Men in this field resent women colleagues" (p. 95).

The feminine image that women in our society are expected to maintain contains a variety of noncharacteristics: "lack of aggressiveness, lack of personal involvement (unless it is for the benefit of a family member), and lack of ambitious drive" (Epstein 1970, p. 22). Riesman (1965) presented another popular conception of women: "From their early days of school they are more people-oriented than boys. They are more adept at the social side of life, and they have fewer distractions from it, whether in sports, or hot-rodding, or science fiction, or many other things which are not exclusively, but largely, boys' hobbies" (p. 425).

These notions of feminine characteristics and interests may affect the fields that women do or do not choose. Feldman (1974), who found that college students readily differentiated between "masculine" and "feminine" fields on a seven-point scale, concludes that "because fields are viewed as feminine, women enter them, and because women are in them, they are viewed as feminine" (p. 45). Women are drawn into fields that are more teaching- than research-oriented: "Fields with strong teaching orientation offer less prestige, power, and privilege than research-oriented fields" (pp. 59-60). Such fields include the humanities, social work, education, and library science.

College women also may be handicapped by their lack of training in mathematics. In a random sample of freshmen admitted to the University of California, Berkeley (UCB), in fall 1972, Sells (1973a) found that 57 percent of the boys had taken four years of high school math (first-year algebra, geometry, second-year algebra, trigonometry and solid geometry) compared with 8 percent of the girls. "The four-year math sequence is required for admission to Math 1A, Chem

1A, and Physics 1A at Berkeley. These courses are required for
majoring in every field at the University except the 'traditionally
female' (and hence lower paying) fields of humanities, social sciences,
education, and social welfare" (p. 43).

Astin (1969) found that, "compared with the typical woman
graduate, the woman who goes on to get a doctorate has a strong
tendency to take her undergraduate major in a field considered masculine and more intellectually demanding" (p. 38). Because of the
tendency of most women to follow society's norms, Rossi (1965) refers
to women who venture into traditionally masculine fields as "pioneers."

The limitation that socialization has placed upon women was
summarized by Bem and Bem (1971): "As long as a woman's socialization does not nurture her uniqueness, but treats her only as a member
of a group on the basis of some assumed average characteristic, she
will not be prepared to realize her own potential in the way that the
values of individuality and self-fulfillment imply that she should"
(p. 22).

ADMISSIONS CRITERIA

Colleges and universities obviously cannot be held accountable
for socialization factors that discourage women from applying to
graduate school. However, for the women who do apply, the criteria
by which admissions committees make their selections are of critical
importance. Ideally, members of admissions committees base their
judgments on characteristics independent of sex. Accepted measures
of potential for academic success include evaluation of past performance (grades and letters of recommendation) plus a standardized test,
the Graduate Record Examination (GRE), to predict academic ability.

One problem in determining whether graduate admissions committees are using sex-neutral selection criteria is that most decisions
are made by individual departments in closed-door meetings. Few
departments have documented their selection criteria; they generally
provide no specific written information on why particular candidates
were denied admission.

Investigators have questioned the selection process, suggesting
that women are not admitted in sufficient proportions if merit is the
most important selection variable (Harris 1970; Sells 1973b; Roby
1973). Other factors influencing selection decisions include information and attitudes about group norms. Past performance of women and
men may be compared to predict student motivation, time to degree
completion, and use of the degree in future employment. Because this
information may influence a committee's decision, an investigation of
possible discrimination must look at reported differences between men
and women in attrition and time required to earn a degree, in motivation,

and in productivity of graduates in employment, as well as at measures
of student ability.

A frequent complaint, that women need better academic qualifications than men to be admitted to graduate school, is generally based
on studies indicating that women have higher grade point averages
(GPA) than men from high school through graduate school. Harmon
(1965), after looking at the high school records of Ph.D. recipients,
concluded that women doctorates are superior to their men counterparts on all measures derived from high school records in all fields of
specialization. However, this is evidence concerning the successful
degree recipients, not the full set of applicants. The Cooperative
Institutional Research Program's annual survey of college freshmen,
sponsored jointly by the American Council on Education (ACE) and the
University of California, Los Angeles, has been cited by Hole and
Levine (1971, p. 318) to show that a greater percentage of girls than
boys have good grades: "for the class entering college in 1968 over
40% of the girls admitted to four-year colleges have B+ or better
averages in high school whereas only 18% of the boys had such
grades." Similar findings are reported for college grades. A survey
by the Carnegie Commission (Feldman 1974) showed that "undergraduate GPA's of B+ or better were achieved by 37% of the men,
compared to 52% of the women. Thus, the greater proportion of men
are entering graduate school with lower undergraduate averages than
their (fewer in number) female counterparts" (p. 18). Roby (1973)
cited ACE data indicating that both high school and college records of
women graduate students are superior to those of men, concluding that
"though admittedly indirect evidence, the data reviewed here strongly
suggest that institutions of higher education maintain higher standards
for the admission of women than they do for men" (p. 42).

Comparative Graduate Record Examination (GRE) scores of men
and women have not indicated the greater ability of women students.
(Chapter 2 presents data on GRE scores of applicants.) Rees (1974)
reported that at Yale, where men had higher GRE scores than women,
women rated higher than men by a small margin on verbal ability,
while men rated higher than women by a large margin on quantitative
ability. At the City University of New York, women also rated higher
in verbal and men higher in quantitative, but the margins were about
equal. "Although rarely discussed in the literature, the use of test
scores as admissions criteria helps men compensate for the better
high school records of women," according to Cross (1974, p. 36).
This lack of emphasis on the GRE may result from the difficulty in
obtaining GRE information; also this information will not benefit the
cause of women. Since GRE scores are not higher for women than for
men, their admissions compared to men will not be helped by using
this as a criterion. (Evidence that GRE performance for women, unlike
GPA, is not superior to that of men is presented below.)

Not all schools or departments rely on grades or standardized
tests as the primary means for student assessment. A study of

psychology departments by an American Psychological Association
task force found that college grades and test scores were not
emphasized; the two most important criteria for selecting students
were letters of recommendation and personal statements (Solmon 1973).
Although the personal statement provides a fair chance for the candidate to discuss his or her motivation, letters of recommendation are
not necessarily free from sex bias: certain letters, written by men,
contained comments irrelevant to the evaluation of scholarship.
Letters of recommendation for National Science Foundation (NSF)
fellowships, collected by the National Research Council, provide
examples of sex-biased statements:

> "I kept wondering how a girl could be so smart."
> "The effect of her being married is, of course, the big
>   unknown."
> "If she were single and plain, I would expect her to be
>   an outstanding Ph.D."
> "Miss K . . . is also musically and structurally gifted."
> "I think she'd make some young anthropologist a good
>   wife."

Such comments are alleged to perpetuate the impression that
scholarly ambition is not a feminine virtue, distracting the reader
from the more important concerns of student motivation and learning
capacity.

Those who objected to current admissions procedures thought
that women's acceptance rates would improve if grades were the most
important criterion. Cross (1974) cited a survey of admissions policies
indicating that most departments assign the greatest weight to the
undergraduate record (p. 41). Women's superior grades put them in a
strong competitive position, but the best they can hope for now is to
be accepted in the same proportion in which they apply. Because
women applicants are a more highly self-selected group than men
applicants, the proportion of women accepted should reflect their
superior qualifications. Scott (1970) noted that women should expect
to be accepted in higher proportions, especially in areas where they
are a minority. Women who apply to traditionally male-dominated
fields, such as medicine, mathematics, physics, and economics, will
do so only because they have exceptional ability and straight A's in
their special fields. "Thus while women graduate students are, to
start with, a much more highly preselected group than are men graduate
students, the women entering male-dominated fields will be a very
preselected group indeed" (p. 287). Probably, "whenever a certain
graduate or professional program regularly admits only a small and
uniform percentage of women students, a quota system may be pre-
sumed to be operating." Roby (1973) attacked the "equal rejection"
theory in which "women applicants are separated from men applicants,

and an equal proportion of each sex category is accepted which means that women are not judged on an equal competitive basis with men. Since women have better academic records than men, and in traditionally masculine fields like medicine and law only the very best women even apply, it is clear that the 'equal rejection' procedure discriminates against women" (p. 43).

Needed is information about the men and women who are not admitted to graduate schools, as well as about successful applicants. Clearly, the measures to evaluate student ability and motivation are far from perfect, but it is necessary to know how admissions committees compare men and women on certain standards to prove discrimination. Without this knowledge, "it might be that graduate admissions committees base their decisions on what they generally observe to be true, even though many cases do not conform with what is generally believed to be the typically observed behavior. However, what they observe may well be biased, and what they (perhaps unconsciously) fail to observe may be important" (Solmon 1973, p. 310).

ATTRITION AND TIME REQUIRED TO EARN A DEGREE

Ph.D. production is a costly endeavor when university resources and student opportunity costs are considered (Breneman 1970). For this reason, departments reviewing admissions applications may consider the likelihood that a student will complete the degree in a minimal time period. "It is said that so many things can happen to interfere with a woman's commitment to graduate study—marriage, pregnancy, moving away with her husband, and so on—that a man is a better bet for a long-range contribution to society. Although such practice seems unjust to the individual (since no one can predict which man or woman will complete the degree), many regard it as a more responsible use of graduate training resources" (Cross 1974, p. 42).

Little information is available to date on degree completion rates for women and men. Most studies suggest that a greater percentage of women drop out of graduate school and that women take longer to complete degrees. When Sells (1973b) interpreted Mooney's data on Woodrow Wilson Fellows who entered graduate school in 1958-63, she analyzed for dropouts rather than completed degrees. She found that 44 percent of the men and 64 percent of the women had dropped out of the program after eight years. Stark (1967), who studied attrition and duration of Ph.D. candidates at UCB, concluded that women are indeed unlikely to succeed in graduate school. He reported low completion rates for women in English, history, and political science, remarking that "when one considers the almost total failure of these three departments to get their female students through to the doctorate, the fact that chemistry got 31 percent of its women through seems a stunning accomplishment" (p. 24). Rees (1974) also cited statistics indicating that women either drop out or take longer than men to complete a degree. "Rossi, in her special study of graduate sociology departments, found that although 39% of the students at the University of Chicago were women, over a nine-year period only 18% of the Ph.D. graduates were women. And at Wisconsin, although 28% of the graduate students were women, only 4% of the degrees awarded went to women" (p. 182). These figures may not accurately reflect the situation, however, because, as Rossi pointed out, some women who intend to stop with a master's degree in social welfare may appear to be doctoral dropouts.

Patterson and Sells (1973) reported that "the literature on graduate school attrition reveals two constant patterns: Women are more likely to drop out and students of both sexes are more likely to fail to complete doctoral programs in the humanities and social sciences than in the physical sciences" (p. 84). However, the factors operating to produce different attrition rates for men and women have not been adequately addressed.

Investigators have looked at such variables as field of study, financial aid, student employment, and marital status for clues on why students drop out, but the relationship of these factors to the women's higher dropout rate is only speculative. Harris (1970) referred to studies that indicate "the attrition rate for both sexes is higher in humanities and social sciences than in physical sciences and professional schools," concluding that "since women are more often found in the former two fields, their overall attrition rate is higher than that of men, but when the figures are compared by field, the differences are small." She presented the University of Chicago study's breakdown by field, which shows that "the overall difference in attrition rates of men and women graduate students was in fact rather minimal, with women actually having a lower attrition rate than men in the humanities" (p. 286).

Financial aid is important to a graduate student's persistence. A survey of women Ph.D.s in Oklahoma by Mitchell and Alciatore (1970) supported the contention that women could earn the degree in less time if they were aided financially. Both income loss and the cost of acquiring the doctorate are significantly related to the time taken to receive the degree. Some delays due to family responsibilities are related to finances. Stark (1967) showed that financial aid and lower attrition rates are significantly related. In comparing the amount of financial aid from different departments, Stark reported that only one-third of the students in English, history, and political science receive financial aid through a teaching or research assistantship, fellowship, scholarship, lectureship, or associateship, compared with 90 percent of chemistry students. Since chemistry students have a much higher success rate than students in other fields, Stark concluded that "if you support an historian as well as you support a chemist, he is as likely as the chemist to succeed in graduate school. Or, conversely, if you starve a chemist the way most students in English are starved (and also deny him the learning experience provided by a research assistantship) the chemist turns out to be as likely as the English student to become a graduate school dropout" (p. 32). Astin's study (1975) of dropping out by undergraduates revealed not only the amount but also the type of aid is significant.

The greater availability of financial support in the physical and biological sciences, compared with the social sciences and humanities, at least partly explains differences in attrition between men and women. Women are more likely to be studying in fields where there are fewer fellowships available. This should make it more difficult for them to complete their graduate studies (Harris 1970, p. 286).

Patterson and Sells (1973) were unconvinced that women's higher dropout rate results from financial difficulties. However, they reported that the Mooney study on Woodrow Wilson Fellows tends to support the importance of financial aid. Figures from the Mooney data "very clearly show that the presence of fellowship support for women in their second year of graduate school reduces their dropout rate by more than one-fourth. Second year fellowship is also associated with a lower dropout rate for men, but the difference is not nearly so great" (p. 88). The byproducts of financial aid, emotional support, and experience as a colleague, may be as important to the student's progress as the money. "The slightly higher attrition rates of women graduate students are largely explained by the lack of encouragement and by the actual discouragement experienced by women graduate students for their career plans" (Harris 1970, p. 286).

Breneman (1970), looking at Mooney's study of Woodrow Wilson Fellows, was struck that the success rate varied by school. "The conclusion has to be that there are obstacles in the way of acquiring a Ph.D. related to sex, field of study, and graduate school, etc. which are not easily overcome simply by injecting more money" (p. 120). Davis (1962) loosely interpreted his findings as indexes of involvement in graduate school versus involvement in the world outside. Areas of involvement in his study include motivation (researchers have low dropout rates; students who do not prefer either teaching or research have high rates), division (natural science students have low dropout rates, humanities students have high rates; social scientists are in the middle), employment (full-time workers have high dropout rates; assistants have low rates; fellows, part-time workers, and those with no employment or fellowship are generally in the middle), and age and family role (older students and fathers have high dropout rates).

Difficulty combining student and family roles may cause more women than men to drop out. Feldman (1974) reported the Carnegie survey finding that "Among married students, 21% of the women as compared with 9% of the men (gamma of sex differences = 0.4444) state that pressure from their spouse will or may cause them to drop out of school" (p. 988). Davis (1962) summarized data on marital status and expectations of graduate students: "Women students have lower marriage rates and higher marriage expectations than men, which suggests that women tend to drop out of graduate school when they get married" (p. 31).

Patterson and Sells (1973) reported on the differential effect of parenthood on women and men graduate students enrolled in one department at UCB: "if a woman was married but had no children, she spent fifty hours a week on household chores. If she was married with children she spent sixty hours on household duties. Single men and women, on the other hand, spent about fifteen to twenty hours on household work a week. Married men, including those with children, devoted less than ten hours a week to housework." They concluded that "it is not surprising then that several studies found marital and family status was the best predictor of women's attrition rate" (pp. 87-88).

The problem of interpreting differential attrition rates for men and women is magnified by the difficulty in collecting reliable information. As Siegel and Carr (1969) noted: "Data on attrition and enrollment are difficult to obtain and interpret because of the geographic mobility of American students—they frequently move from one educational setting to another without in fact interrupting the progress of their educational careers" (p. 6). The educational structure does not yet accommodate this mobility, and women students are victimized more than men: "We have yet to deal realistically with the portability of credits. And this problem is exaggerated for women who generally move, not at their convenience, but when husbands have completed a given segment of education" (Cross 1974, p. 47). (Chapter 4 presents data on geographic mobility patterns of students of each sex and the interinstitutional mobility of doctorate recipients.)

Women generally complete their degrees later in life than men for a variety of reasons, such as temporarily terminating training after graduation to work for financial reasons or to break the academic routine, interrupting training to marry and have children, and extending training by attending college part time (Astin 1969). Ultimately, many of these women complete a degree, but such delays account for the average 12-year lapse between graduation and Ph.D. completion. (This time lapse and the actual number of years spent in graduate training are differentiated below.) Women in the Mitchell and Alciatore (1970) sample thought they could have begun their graduate study earlier. "More than 60% of all women in this study, and over 80% of those who exceeded the median time lapse from B.A. to Ph.D., indicated they would begin their doctoral study earlier in their lives if they were to do it again. In retrospect they were able to see ways in which they could have managed their lives so as to have achieved the degree at an earlier time" (p. 538). Mitchell and Alciatore concluded that "greater cultural expectations regarding women doctorates and improvement of guidance and counseling may encourage women to earn the doctor's degree earlier in their lives so as to realize greater gains for themselves and for society" (p. 538).

The pattern of women's dropout rates does not differ significantly from that of men at certain schools. Rees (1974) reported that "our records seem to present strong evidence that, at least at the City University of New York, attrition rates are about the same for men as for women and women do complete the degree though it takes them almost a half year longer than men" (p. 183). According to Sells (1973b), the difference in men's and women's attrition rates at UCB has been diminishing since women students have organized on their own behalf in women's caucuses: "The long-standing sex difference of 20 percentage points in dropouts was gradually reduced to zero in the wake of women's increasing efforts to seize their own autonomy," she noted (p. 10). Attrition has decreased because "faculty are beginning to learn not to impose expectations and stereotypes based on the behavior of women in the 1960's on women of the 1970's."

STUDENT MOTIVATION

The student's level of commitment to graduate study is presumably an important consideration for graduate admissions committees. Although grades, letters of recommendation, and the candidate's personal statement are measures of motivation, subjective opinions also may influence the committee's evaluation. Arguments that women are not as committed to graduate study as men have been challenged by individuals who think evidence does not support this generalization.

As a spokesman for educators who think many women pursue higher education for reasons other than scholarship, Lewis (1969) outlined a variety of nonacademic motives: to please others (a bright girl who continues under pressure from a favored instructor); to remain in a secure environment (arising from fear of the outside world or desire to find a husband); and to mark time until her husband graduates. Commitment to a scholarly field is a primary motive for men but not for most women, he found:

> Too many young women are casually enrolling in graduate
> schools across the country without having seriously con-
> sidered the obligation which they are assuming by request-
> ing that such expenditures be made for them. And they are
> not alone to blame. Equally at fault are two groups of
> faculty: a) undergraduate instructors who encourage their
> female students to apply without also helping them consider

the commitment that such an act implies, and b) graduate admissions committees who blithely admit girls with impressive academic records into their graduate programs without looking for other evidence that the applicant has made a sincere commitment to graduate study (p. 33).

Rees (1974) quoted Virgil K. Whitaker, former dean of the Stanford graduate school, who held a similar view:

A much thornier problem, especially in the humanities, is provided by the young ladies. They mostly profess an undy-ing devotion to learning, at least on their applications. But for many of them the need to find a place in the world that plagues both sexes is complicated, to speak quite bluntly, by the need to find a man. A fellowship provides support while they continue the hunt . . . there is . . . ample statistical support for the proposition that the hard-pressed American taxpayer, or even the generous donor is not getting his money's worth out of women graduate stu-dents if Ph.D.'s practicing their profession is the goal (p. 179).

Graham (1970) saw the period from age 18 to 25, when most young men are preparing themselves for a career, as a difficult time for women students. "Some young women are able to do graduate work and do it well in these years, but few pass through this period without serious qualms about the desirability of planning for a demanding pro-fessional life" (p. 1285).

That they are not taken seriously may be an impediment for women students. "The first thing that male students do is to suspect the intentions of women. The suspicion is generally that women come to graduate school to look for a man, not a degree," according to Fox (1970, p. 33). Women students do not receive positive support; it is considered unusual if they continue for their Ph.D.'s and no tragedy if they drop out. Graduate men, according to Fox, think women have the option to leave any time they want; they don't have to be there. "Women scholars are not taken seriously and cannot look forward to a normal professional career," according to Caplow and McGee (1958). "This bias is part of the much larger pattern which determines the utilization of women in our economy. It is not peculiar to the academic world, but it does blight the prospects of female scholars" (p. 194).

Sells (1973b) conducted a pilot study at Berkeley in which faculty responded to the item, "The women graduate students in this department are not as dedicated as the men," and women graduate students responded to the item, "The professors in my department don't take female graduate students seriously." She found "large and statistically significant differences in faculty attitudes toward women, across disciplines, and most importantly, between faculty attitudes and student perceptions in History, English, Political Science, and Sociology." Faculty opinions ranged from 19 to 49 percent who believe women students are less dedicated, and students from 28 to 55 percent that women students are not taken seriously. Yet, "it is not clear whether students pick up and reflect faculty expectations with respect to their seriousness, or whether students behave in a manner which elicits expectations of lack of seriousness" (p. 8).

What appears to be less motivation by women students may actually be lack of self-confidence and a less positive self-image. Feldman (1974), in his survey for the Carnegie Commission, found that women have less confidence in their ability to do original work:

> Women appear to be not as dedicated as men. However, given a close relationship with a professor or given a more positive self-image, women are just as likely as men to manifest signs of dedication. . . . We cannot establish that believing females to be less dedicated is an indication of blind prejudice. The belief becomes part of a cycle— a professor sees that women are not as dedicated as men and pays less attention to them. Paying less attention to them results in women becoming less dedicated; hence, the belief is upheld (p. 123).

While some women scholars lack confidence in their abilities, the problem may arise because the academic environment is structured for men. "They [women students] sometimes feel a personal inadequacy, and I often see my own students coming to the conclusion that they lack ability in various fields when, in fact, what they lack is the ability to structure their thinking in the way that men have defined their spheres" (Riesman 1965, p. 427).

If women students are assumed to be less motivated than men students, they may be involved in fewer relationships with men students and professors who encourage them to continue in school. Husbands (1972) cited studies of graduate students in which "many researchers have emphasized the importance of reference groups in forming and reinforcing professional self-concepts" (p. 266). Married women students are at a particular disadvantage. "Married women graduate students in Erbe's national sample knew fewer persons in their departments than did men or single women; yet knowing many people in one's department was related to definite intentions to get the doctorate" (pp. 266-67).

Numerous studies have attempted to determine whether marriage has a different impact on the motivation of men and women graduate students. Feldman (1974) reported that marriage is generally a positive influence for men and a negative influence for women, stating that divorced women and married men have the greatest academic success

(p. 136). Graham (1970), however, cites studies indicating that women who are married when they receive a Ph.D. are more capable academically than their unmarried women contemporaries. (The effects of marriage on men and women students who have received the doctorate are considered below.)

Marriage may limit women's aspirations in that women seldom seek a higher academic level than their husbands. According to Feldman (1974),

> Traditionally, it has been deemed unacceptable in our society for a woman to dominate her husband in any way—including educationally. Thus, married women are freer to pursue postgraduate training if their spouses have also done so. No such limitations exist for men. Less than a quarter of married male students have spouses with graduate education as compared with over half of the married graduate women. These differences obtain for all age groups—even women who return to graduate school after the age of 40 are more likely to have spouses with graduate education than men of a similar age (p. 127).

In Astin's (1969) sample of married women Ph.D.'s, 51 percent reported that their husbands also have a doctorate and an additional 12 percent were married to men with a professional degree. Only 10 percent were married to men who were not college graduates. Simon et al. (1967) also noted that "the Ph.D. places greater restrictions on the woman's choice of spouse than it does on the man's" (p. 223).

For whatever reasons, it has generally been confirmed that fewer women than men graduate students or Ph.D.'s are married. Astin (1969) compared the marriage rate of women Ph.D.'s with the population in general to find that only 55 percent (59 percent if nuns were excluded) had been married, compared with 86 percent of other women in the age group (40 to 44 years old).

Feldman (1974) suggested that "the tendency of married or divorced women to be older than men of similar status reflects the fact that women are more constrained by the role of spouse. Unlike women, men do not have to wait until their children are raised or until their spouse has an established career to continue in graduate school" (p. 129). Since about three-fourths of the married Ph.D.'s in her sample were married before completing graduate training, H. Astin (1969) concluded that some women can successfully combine wife and student roles. The women in Astin's sample had fewer children born later in life than those in the general population. Simon et al. (1967) reported that, although 70 percent of the married women Ph.D.'s in their sample had at least one child, this percentage was lower than that for men (90 percent of the married men had children).

The possible constraints of marriage on women may be reflected in the greater number enrolled as part-time students. Feldman (1974) found that "while marriage reduced the frequency of full-time enrollment for both men and women, it is more likely to reduce it for women than for men" (p. 984). About one-half of the married men in his sample were full-time students, compared with less than one-third of the married women.

POSTGRADUATE EMPLOYMENT AND PRODUCTIVITY

Since the reputations of colleges and universities depend to some extent on the success of their graduates, candidates for admissions may be evaluated for their potential to be productive and visible in postgraduate employment. If it is assumed that women will invest more energy in their family lives than in productive employment, the decision to admit a high proportion of women to graduate school may be seen as disadvantageous by an institution. However, educators do not agree on which activities are productive, and evidence suggests that women Ph.D. recipients do utilize their degrees.

Astin (1969) reported that "the higher a woman's educational attainment, the more likely she is to be in the labor force; the 1960 census data show that women's labor force participation is directly proportionate in their education, independent of age" (p. 2). The Astin survey indicated that not only are 91 percent of all women who received their doctorates in 1957 and 1958 employed but their employment patterns are also stable; less than one-fifth of the fully employed have ever interrupted their postdoctoral careers and these interruptions have been for an average total of about 14 months. "Once a woman decides to invest herself, her time, and her energy in pursuit of specialized training, the likelihood of her maintaining a strong career interest and commitment is very high" (p. 149).

Simon et al. (1967) also found that a high proportion of women with a Ph.D. are "practicing their trade." Practically all the unmarried women in their sample and 87 percent of the married women without children work full time. Among the married women with children, 60 percent work full time, while 25 percent work part time. In Mitchell and Alciatore's (1970) survey of Oklahoma women Ph.D.'s, "Seven of the women had reached retirement age. Among the remaining women there was an almost incredible rate of 99 percent employment" (p. 536). The high employment rate of women Ph.D.'s in these studies demonstrates the trend toward greater labor force participation of academic women. In an earlier survey by Radcliffe (1956) of its graduates, 31 percent of the respondents were classified as "nonworkers," a greater unemployment rate than indicated in more current studies.

Employers today may be more receptive to hiring qualified women than in the past. Certainly, more information is needed to determine how many women graduates are seeking and not finding jobs that utilize their training. Roby (1973) cited a 1970 study by John Creager that suggests women graduate students are seriously preparing for employment: "70% of both men and women graduate students endorsed the view that 'career will take second place to family obligations' in their lives" (p. 50).

The student's future employment is, to some degree, determined by his or her department:

Since the department is a major source of information concerning job opportunities, this factor is, to a considerable extent, under departmental control. For example, professors may know that women Ph.D.'s are discriminated against for job placement; this knowledge may cause many women graduate students to quit the program. If the department has some reason for wanting these students to remain in the program, then the department will carefully avoid discussion of job opportunities (Breneman 1970, p. 33).

Harris (1970) claimed that "the informal grapevine of job openings from department to department across the country" is detrimental to women. "The cliche opening, 'Do you know a good man for the job?' reflects a continuous but largely unconscious discrimination against women" (p. 292).

Surveys have indicated that women Ph.D.'s do not think discrimination interferes with their attainment of a job as much as with their advancement on the job. In Mitchell and Alciatore's (1970) sample, two-fifths (42.4 percent) of the women reported they had not experienced any discrimination since receiving the Ph.D. A slightly larger percentage (48.8 percent) said they had felt some discrimination in the following areas: promotion or salary or both (24.95 percent), nepotism regulations (6.2 percent), administrative positions (4.5 percent), and a general atmosphere of discrimination (10.2 percent). Over one-third of the women in Astin's sample believed that discriminatory practices had adversely affected their careers. The forms of discrimination mentioned most often are lower salary schedules for women and differential treatment over promotion, tenure, and seniority.

Women's advancement in academe has been thwarted by the common assumption that women are more inclined toward teaching than research. H. Astin (1969) commented that "women are less productive than men with respect to publications of scholarly writing, and this sex difference may reflect the basic differences in the attitudes, values, and interests of the two sexes" (p. 93). The typical work activities of Astin's sample were divided; half the time was spent teaching, one-fourth in research, and one-fourth in administration and service to clients. Simon et al. (1967) reported that "when respondents were asked to describe the work they do, and were given choices of 'teaching,' 'research,' 'both,' or 'other,' we found that while there was considerable variation by field, there was no consistent pattern between the sexes" (p. 224).

Some studies suggested that women's involvement in research equals that of men. Simon et al. (1967) showed that married women Ph.D.'s employed full time publish slightly more than men or unmarried women Ph.D.'s, a finding that contradicts Feldman's (1974) report that married women publish less than married men. Cross (1974) cited Creager to show that field of study has more to do with publishing than the sex of the student: Scientists are productive and educators are not. As mentioned above, women are involved in fewer research-oriented fields.

Some evidence has indicated that the quality of publications by women is not lower than that of men. Lindsey Harmon of the National Research Council, who has produced some unpublished tabulations with publications and citations indexes of the Institute for Scientific Information, found that even though women doctorates publish fewer articles and books, their works are cited more often than those of men. Considering that citations come from two sources—former teachers and colleagues, and those who actually use the publication—this finding is noteworthy. If former teachers and colleagues favor men, the larger number of citations of women's work probably reflects greater use in new research.

Another explanation for women's lack of scholarly production is that women more often hold jobs at teaching institutions than at research universities (Cross 1974). Simon et al. (1967) supported the contention that women are less likely than men to be employed at universities. "Among those respondents who work in academic institutions, the proportion of unmarried women compared to men who are employed at colleges rather than universities (state or private) is higher in the sciences and social sciences. In the humanities and education there is little difference by sex. There is also some tendency for married women to be employed at private rather than public universities" (p. 224). Astin (1969) also found that place of employment for women Ph.D.'s varies by field. Most of the Astin population is employed in small colleges or universities: women in humanities and social science are likely to be in higher educational settings; women in education are probably in junior colleges; natural scientists are most often found in government, industry, or nonprofit organizations.

QUALITY OF THE GRADUATE SCHOOL

The quality of the graduate school has implications for future employment. Berelson (1960) saw the graduate school as

> one of the most important distributors of talent in American life. Just as a person's eventual position in society depends on the class he was born into as well as on his own talent, so his eventual position in higher education depends on the standing of the (parental) institution where he took his doctorate as well as his scientific or scholarly capabilities. In each case, a good deal depends on what step of the ladder you start from (p. 109).

Few studies have attempted to discern whether men and women students attend graduate schools of equal quality. Berelson reported that, by and large, women receive their doctorates from universities equal in quality to those from which men receive their degrees. About the same proportion of women students (47 percent) as men (43 percent) receive their doctorates from the top 12 universities. Whether women are admitted to the highest-quality graduate schools in the same proportion as men is explored below.

Another question is whether women and men who apply to graduate schools come from undergraduate schools of similar academic status, and whether the quality of their undergraduate training influences their graduate performance. Stark (1967), trying to determine whether the quality of an undergraduate institution affected the probability that the student would complete the Ph.D., found that quality mattered in chemistry but not in other departments. In the chemistry department at UCB, proportions earning Ph.D.'s systematically decline from highest-quality undergraduate (91 percent obtained Ph.D.'s) to students from obscure institutions (50 percent earned Ph.D.'s). Stark did not report these data by sex, although the majority of chemistry students probably are men.

Harris (1970) reported that

> sex-segregated education does not benefit women. The Gourman Institute ratings for all women's schools are at least 200 points (on an 800 scale, 400 being accreditation level) below those of their supposedly equivalent men's schools, with Catholic schools collecting the lowest ratings of all. . . . Even at the best-known women's schools, the smaller endowment, more limited facilities, and smaller range of courses, especially in male-dominated fields, affect all women students (p. 293).

Because the best graduate schools can be more selective in their admissions, the quality of the student's undergraduate institution may be a screening device. In a similar manner, employers may determine the eligibility of applicants by the reputation of the graduate school. Thus, it is important to learn more about the distribution of men and women students in different quality levels of undergraduate and graduate institutions. (New data on the baccalaureate origins of doctorates are presented below.)

FINANCIAL AID

To determine whether discrimination against women occurs in allocation of financial aid, investigators have examined the same factors involved in women's acceptance rates. Information and attitudes about student ability, motivation, likelihood of completing a degree, and employment potential are important variables in financial aid decisions. Some observers argue that women do not receive a fair share of fellowships or school-related employment, especially when student performance is considered. Others believe that women should be bypassed in favor of men, since their commitment to graduate study and future employment is not as substantial.

On the dynamics of financial aid decisions, Riesman (1965) noted: "One can observe, on committees deciding on graduate fellowships, that there is a tendency, where a girl and a boy have relatively equal records, to choose the boy, on the ground that he's a better bet for manpower since he isn't likely to drop out because of marriage. And therefore he will serve the society and the professor himself as a disciple" (p. 430).

Information on differences in financial aid by sex is not readily available. A survey by the American Association of University Women (AAUW) could not disclose the number of graduate fellowships and their value because "This data was not given in consistent form, was not available, or the item was left blank" (Oltman 1970, p. 9). The present study reveals data on the number of men and women graduate students with aid but it is still virtually impossible to obtain useful data on amount of aid by sex. Bernard (1964), looking at the 1959 National Science Foundation awards, reported that women receive awards in the same proportion that they apply; 12 percent of the applicants were women and 12 percent of the awards went to women. Simon et al. (1967) indicated that women are more likely than men to receive postdoctoral fellowships. These findings were consistent with those of Knapp and Greenbaum (1953), who found that women receive university fellowships somewhat more frequently than men. However, the finding on postdoctoral fellowships might reflect the greater difficulty women have in finding a job on receipt of the Ph.D.

Numerous investigators say that women and men receive financial support from different sources and that women do not receive as much financial aid. Attwood (1972) reported the findings of a study by the American Association of Colleges (AAC) in which 68 different fellowship programs sponsored by 28 government agencies and private foundations provided data on numbers and percentages of women applicants, acceptances, and selection procedures. In 28 percent of the programs, the percentage of women recipients was close to the percentage that applied. In the remaining 45 percent, the percentage of women recipients was significantly higher than that of applicants. Attwood was concerned that far fewer women than men apply or are nominated for fellowships. She projected that "in 1972-73, about 80 percent of the nation's most prestigious fellowships and awards [would] go to men" (p. 2). Astin (1973) reported that women were less likely to receive aid from the government or other institutions and more likely to rely on their own savings or support from their families or spouses.

Roby (1973) reviewed ACE data to expose differences between men's and women's sources of support, saying that graduate men are "somewhat more dependent than women on their own efforts, through employment and use of savings or loans, while women are somewhat more dependent on contributions from their families (most frequently, their husbands)" (p. 48). This financial dependence of women on either husbands or families carries with it some psychological implications of emotional indebtedness:

If women depend more on family support than do men, it may be daughters in lower middle class and working class families are especially penalized compared to their brothers. Not only may such families have lowered the educational aspirations of their daughters to a greater extent than their sons, but they may also consider it appropriate for sons to work their way through college, but inappropriate for their daughters to do so (p. 48).

Several studies have examined the differential effect of marital status or family role on the financial standing of men and women graduate students. In the Carnegie survey reported by Feldman (1974), 60 percent of married men said their wives' jobs provide a source of income; 74 percent of married women graduate students stated that their husbands' jobs were a source of income. Feldman (1974) said that marital status does not appear to affect the granting of financial aid. "The general pattern is that men are more likely to receive fellowships. Decisions concerning financial aid may take into account sex but probably not marital status" (p. 136). Davis (1962) outlined a variety of financial situations: Single students have low incomes, low income needs, and seldom work full time. Married women tend to have high incomes and be supported by a working husband. Husbands also tend

to have high incomes and high income needs and are generally partially
dependent on the earnings of a working wife. Fathers have the highest
income needs and often work full time to compensate for the loss of
their wives' earnings. Davis saw fathers as the only group with financial difficulties; their income sources divert their attention from their
studies.

Stark (1967) has suggested that the type and amount of aid a
student receives depends on his or her department. Astin (1969) also
found that financial aid varies by field of study. Women in the natural
sciences are far more likely than those in other fields to receive stipend
support through assistantships or fellowships during graduate training,
while women in education tend to bear the costs of graduate training
themselves. Davis (1962), too, noted that natural science students
have a distinct advantage over social science and humanities students,
regardless of the type of stipend. He pointed out that Ph.D. candidates
have an advantage over master's candidates for most types of stipends.
Since women tend toward fields that offer less aid and are more frequently
master's candidates (NSF) data) than men, these factors may be more
relevant to the determination of financial aid than sex.

Davis (1962) shared Attwood's conclusion that women are far less
likely to apply for stipends than men. While Davis did not speculate
on why women fail to apply for aid, Attwood (1972) proposed that women
might not hear of funds because information often spreads informally in
departments but women are not in these channels. Fields with higher
participation by women, such as humanities and social sciences, generally have a higher level of women financial aid applicants. The highly
self-selected group of women who apply for financial aid is extremely
qualified; women students may have to demonstrate greater proficiency
than men to receive stipends.

Because many fellowships require that students be enrolled full
time (Attwood 1972), women who combine part-time studies with family
responsibilities do not qualify. Roby (1973) said, "Those who are part-
time students are almost automatically cut off from any chance for
financial assistance" (p. 50). The percentage of women and men
enrolled as part-time students is similar, but the full-time status
restriction is a coercive measure that discourages women who would
like to attend school part time. Age requirements for fellowships also
penalize women who want to return to school after their children have
grown.

Cohen and Mesrop (1972) pointed out that women are less likely
to take out federal loans. "Why is it that in the years from 1966-1971,
only 37 percent of the borrowers under the federal program were women?"
(p. 71), they asked. Roby (1973) suggested that women students hesitate to borrow heavily against their future earnings since they can
expect to earn lower wages than men. Since it is more difficult for
women to secure bank loans than men, federal loans must be more
accessible to women students.

Astin (1975) has shown that for undergraduates the type of aid is a crucial factor affecting the probability of dropping out. This finding probably applies to graduate students also. Campus-related work (work-study, research assistantships) has the greatest effect on preventing dropping out. Loans have the most negative impact. Packages of aid are less desirable than aid of a single type. Hence, more study is needed on differences in types of aid to graduate students of each sex, along with research on numbers receiving aid and the amounts.

INSTITUTIONAL FLEXIBILITY

Various practices, such as the full-time status requirement for fellowships, are attacked by people who want to expand opportunities for women in higher education. An important step in alleviating de facto discrimination against women is to make institutions more receptive to the variety of life situations of students.

Related to the old-fashioned notion that education is reserved for the young who can spend full time at it are a host of practices and requirements that are grounded more in tradition than in logic. Why should scholarship and loan aid be so commonly restricted to full-time students? Do residency requirements and regulations that call for continuous enrollment serve a purpose so valuable that we are justified in shutting out students whose life circumstances prohibit meeting them? Why must an individual's academic load be determined by the institution rather than by the learner? (Cross 1974, p. 48).

Because some graduate departments either do not accept or attempt to discourage candidates older than 35, they limit opportunities for both women and men who have not followed the traditional academic pattern. The many women who interrupt their education to have children are particularly vulnerable to age restrictions. Discouraging part-time study is another practice that is not directed against women, but it operates to their disadvantage. Institutions with lower quality ratings have more part-time students than institutions with higher quality ratings (Feldman 1974). Thus, women who want to attend school part time may be more inclined toward lower-quality schools where part-time study is more widely accepted.

Lack of child-care facilities prevents many women from enrolling in graduate school. Roby (1973) cited a study by the Department of Health, Education and Welfare in 1968 in which "women who planned but were not attending graduate school indicated that the availability of child-care facilities topped the list of the factors they considered most

important as a condition to graduate study" (p. 53). The AAUW survey
(Oltman 1970) revealed that among the 454 schools surveyed, only 22
(or 5 percent) provided day-care services for women with small children.
Policies on pregnancy, residence requirements, and birth control
counseling also varied greatly. Large public institutions with medical
resources and a heterogeneous student population are more likely to
have liberal policies and to provide special services to married and
pregnant women students. "On the other hand, small schools with less
than 1,000 students do not have diversified special facilities, but
appear to make up for this in more individualized treatment—counseling,
needed adjustments, and scholarships. Private schools show a similar
trend" (p. 14). "Although this AAUW survey found that 95 percent of
the colleges claimed to offer opportunities for older women to complete
degrees, a follow-up determined that only half of these institutions
made any concessions in the rate of work, class hours, or customary
academic practices to meet the needs of mature women" (Cross 1972,
p. 7).

The many women who return to college after age 30 are a more
important potential resource for society than young women, since they
are more motivated and more likely to "make direct use of their education than will the college girl in her early twenties" (Lewis 1968, p.
213). It is

> inconsistent that colleges would put roadblocks in the way
> of the older woman who wants to return to school, but this
> is in fact what most of them do. Among the handicaps which
> the older woman faces is the loss of undergraduate credits
> which were obtained too long ago, the scheduling of classes
> at times which conflict with family responsibilities, and age
> limits in many graduate and professional programs. Perhaps
> these problems cannot be entirely eliminated, but few schools
> have yet made a serious effort to minimize them and to give
> the returning housewife a break (p. 213).

Many observers contended that the college environment, which
ignores the special needs of graduate women, is debilitating to the
psychological well-being of these women. The graduate school
experience often alienates men, too, but this fact does not remedy
the problems of women students. Alienation arises from the student's
sense of powerlessness. Sells (1973b) told of a pilot project at
Berkeley that brought women together to define their problems in graduate school and find solutions:

> The major insight arising from the group process was the
> recognition by the women involved that their feelings were
> in fact not individual, and even more importantly, that
> they were not limited to students in their own department.

Recognition of these feelings as pervasive characteristics
of graduate student life seems to have made it possible to
deal with them more effectively (p. 3).

Bernard (1964) also saw the graduate school atmosphere as hard-
nosed: "There is not only an absence of a nurturing aspect in the format
of the great graduate universities, but a positive rejection of such an
attitude, a tough-minded approach to learning which they prize. A
latent function of discrimination against women is, in fact, to keep
learning tough" (p. 141). Rather than teaching graduate women to cope
with an inhospitable environment, most protesters advocate tempering
the forces that isolate students, particularly women students.

STUDENT/FACULTY RELATIONSHIPS

The student's feeling of belonging can be facilitated or under-
mined by his or her graduate advisers. The relationship between the
graduate student and his mentor has a special significance:

The relationship, whatever form it may take, is especially
sensitive because so much of the graduate student's future
career depends on it. Because he has not yet been tested,
the graduate student is not sure of himself; he is in a
peculiarly difficult stage of his professional career, a fact
which magnifies the ordinary human relations problems that
arise in any situation where people interact (Bernard 1964,
p. 140).

The predominance of men faculty members may cause problems
for women graduate students more than for men. Sexual ambiguity
causes tension in the cross-sex relationships. The definition of roles
is a potential problem for both the man professor and woman student,
while a collegial relationship may develop comfortably between two
men (Fox 1970). Since this relationship is so vital to the student's
progress, it is unfortunate if women students are handicapped.
    Two factors that seem to have the greatest effect on graduate
school performance are the student's self-image and relationship with
professors (Feldman 1974, p. 121). An area of disadvantage for women
is the quality of interaction with faculty and perceived faculty attitudes.
Holmstrom and Holmstrom (1974) stated that a larger percentage of men
students interact informally with professors. Also, 21 percent of the
men and 31 percent of the women students thought professors do not
take women graduate students seriously.
    Sells (1973b) found large sex differences in student responses to
the question, "Does the professor with whom you have the most

academic contact regard you primarily as: a colleague, an apprentice, an employee, or a student?" A University of Chicago study reported by Freeman (1972) showed that 47 percent of the men and 32 percent of the women perceive faculty as supportive of their plans for a career.

The absence of faculty women may deprive women graduate students of valuable contacts. "It is possible that the woman student, observing the underrepresentation of women in high academic positions, decides that the higher intellectual life is 'for men only'" (Husbands 1972, p. 267). Freeman (1972), too, believes that "The result is that few women have examples before them of how to be a female professional" (p. 11). In addition to serving as role models, women teachers might provide special emotional encouragement to women students through close working relationships.

Tidball (1973), in a study of successful women (defined as those appearing in Who's Who), found that a disproportionate number graduated from women's colleges. Since the woman faculty/woman student ratio was strongly and positively correlated with the number of career-successful women graduates for all types of institutions, and since this ratio in the women's colleges was twice as great as that found in the coeducational colleges, she suggested that the relatively greater success of women students from women's colleges derives from their having more effective women role models to identify with and emulate. Further, since the colleges in the study represented all levels of selectivity for both institutional types, the possibility exists that talent loss occurs more frequently in institutions that provide fewer adult women role models for women students. The Tidball study was unable to control for innate ability and it may be that, in earlier years, the most able women attended women's colleges. If these bright women had attended coeducational institutions, they might still have made Who's Who.

Achievement clearly depends upon initial ability and self-esteem. If one observes the women with high ability attending institutions that best stimulate high self-esteem development, it is difficult to distinguish which is more important in contributing to high achievement. Hence the strength of Tidball's results depend upon whether or not the best women went to single-sex institutions. In private correspondence, Tidball has written, "[the] supposition that 'in the earlier years' the brighter women might have attended the women's colleges more frequently would be very hard to substantiate—especially considering that some 70% of women then attended coeducational colleges, that the colleges in the study included many small Roman Catholic institutions (which have not been viewed as especially prestigious places), and that the absolute number of 'achievers' is, of course, greater from the coeducational colleges."

DISCRIMINATION AGAINST FACULTY WOMEN

Women scholars who survive graduate school enter a new area of potential discrimination: the faculty structure. "The higher, the fewer" is a "rule" that explains the funneling process of women in academia (Harris 1970, p. 284). Women who are hired are most frequently in lower ranks. Women are utilized extensively as instructors in the top institutions, averaging 16 percent for all disciplines (Parrish 1962). The rate declines to 10 percent for assistant and associate professors, and to 5 percent for professors. Harris (1970) said that Parrish's percentages of professors, associate professors, assistant professors, and instructors in 1960 have not changed although the number of instructors has. "Nor will they move up in this decade," she noted, "unless academic men learn to accept women at the top rank as well as at the bottom" (p. 290). Further:

> Women earned about 13 percent of all the Ph.D.'s awarded in the 1960's . . . and comprised about 22 percent of the faculty in all institutions of higher education. In all kinds of institutions, however, women are distributed unevenly, clustered in the lower ranks, in part-time positions, and in institutions or programs considered by some to be low-prestige (p. 289).

In a disguised experiment, Simpson (1969) found that employing agents in colleges and universities did exhibit discrimination in hiring women applicants as qualified as men. Identical pairs of resumes for men and women were submitted to employers. Although the employers picked more qualified women over less qualified men, certain subjects (who also showed negative attitudes toward women on the Open Subordination of Women Attitude Scale) picked men over equally qualified women. Nepotism policies account for some women scholars being bypassed in favor of their husbands. Although nepotism regulations have been liberalized in public institutions in the last ten years, little change has occurred in the private sector (Oltman 1970).

Not only are academic women teaching in colleges and universities in the lower professional ranks but they reportedly are not promoted as quickly as men (Hole and Levine 1971). According to Bayer and Astin (1968), a woman is more likely to receive a promotion than higher pay: "It appears that institutions often operate on differential pay scales for women and men whereby they justify the greater salaries for men on the basis of greater economic need on the part of those who are the primary family breadwinner" (pp. 199-200).

In a replication of this study, Bayer and Astin (1975) concluded that higher education still appears to have a long way to go before attaining equity between the sexes. On average, women would appear to merit approximately a one-tenth step in rank promotion in the 1972-73 academic year, and women who are full professors would average an increase for equity of almost $1,700 in their salaries nationally.

Simon et al. (1967) compared mean income by field and sex and found that "men earned noticeably more than women in only one field—education. In other areas, the differences ranged from about $800 in the sciences to less than $400 in the humanities" (p. 227). Women are often channeled into fields that are not particularly well paid (Astin and Bayer 1972).

Part of the discouragement of women graduate students may result from their observation of the difficulties women confront after graduation. The reported inequities in faculty ranks are as difficult to substantiate as the adverse treatment of women in graduate school. It is healthy to examine the system for possible injustices. How these injustices may be remedied is another area to be explored.

RECOMMENDATIONS

Most literature on discrimination against women focuses on areas where discrimination exists. Many authors believe in the cause of women and would admit that they have an emotional as well as scientific involvement in the subject matter. Fewer articles justify the practices and policies that have affected women in higher education. The scarcity of hard data to substantiate discrimination limits the value of many arguments that claim discrimination does or does not exist. Virtually all investigators imply that institutions need to document information on admissions, financial aid, and hiring procedures. The most valuable contribution of the studies thus far is that they point out patterns in higher education that need examination.

Cross (1974) suggested that fact-finding committees be established by colleges to assess local problems and needs. The committees could look into meeting national recognized needs, such as child-care centers, part-time study options, and adequate educational and career counseling for women of all ages. But they could also pay special attention to the full spectrum of local problems (p. 49). Some of the institutional self-studies already conducted are reviewed below.

Statistics for graduate students need to be examined each year for possible discriminatory patterns. Greater efforts to recruit women students must be made by individual campuses. The allotment of financial aid should be investigated as it relates to recruitment and employment opportunities for men and women graduate students. The schools also must concern themselves with aiding both men and women graduates in the initial job search.

Since women have generally not been in leadership positions as students or faculty members, opportunities for advancement must be made available to women (Oltman 1970). The hiring, salary, and promotion opportunities for women faculty need investigation by individual schools. Development of better counseling and more programs to meet the specific needs of women students also is an area for action.

Counseling women in their undergraduate years may help to motivate them to pursue higher levels of education by revealing possible alternatives. Perhaps accommodations for child care and part-time study would encourage more women to begin or complete degrees.

Sandler (1972) outlined university health services for women. Basic elements include medical services, counseling and educational services, and insurance coverage. Campuses that prohibit or discourage pregnant women students or faculty from taking leaves of absence need to re-examine the basis for such rules.

Recent legislation (Executive Order 11246 as amended by 11375; Title VII of the Civil Rights Act of 1964 as amended by the Equal Employment Opportunity Act of 1972; and the Equal Pay Act of 1963 as amended by the Education Amendments of 1972) pressured institutions to examine the status of women students and employees. In essence, these laws forbid discrimination against students and employees in all federally assisted education programs. Universities seeking federal contracts are required to present affirmative action plans and methods to implement them:

> Discrimination may be discovered through the mechanism of the affirmative action plan, which is a projection of remedial steps based on the contractor's own analysis of its work force. If discrimination is found, the contractor's personnel system is reviewed for deficiencies, and the contractor must propose changes in the system and goals and time tables to bring employment up to parity (DHEW 1974, p. 4).

Complaints are directed to the Department of Health, Education, and Welfare, Office for Civil Rights. Because of the large number of complaints, the Equal Employment Opportunity Commission has taken over many cases.

Various solutions have been recommended to improve the ratios of women accepted by graduate schools and hired by universities. Rossi (1973) suggested that, with the current trend toward restricting enrollment, the proportion of women admitted be increased. This way, "the number of women would increase slightly, but the number of men would decline more than 50 percent" (p. 527). Chalmers (1972) offered several other approaches:

> Initially HEW required the University of Michigan to increase the ratio of female admissions to all Ph.D. programs. Another group at Yale University proposed that whenever

the proportion of qualified applicants to a particular graduate department fell below 35 percent, the department would be obliged to actively recruit women applicants. Still another formula proposes that women should be admitted to post-baccalaureate programs in the same ratio as women who complete undergraduate degree programs in the department (school, college or university). Advocates of another solution urge admission of women in the same ratio as they apply (p. 520).

Accepting a fixed formula for admissions and hiring creates new problems. Any inflexible system does not account for the differing interests and abilities of applicants. According to Feldman (1974), "Setting up quotas on the basis of sex, while increasing female representation, is a token gesture and will not eliminate the different training that many women bring to colleges and universities" (p. 137). More information, such as the proportions of each sex that wish to continue their education in different disciplines and professions, is needed before answers can be reached. "It will require the devotion of considerably greater time and attention to criteria for admission, but the effort must be made if we are to rectify the real imbalance that has occurred in the past" (Chalmers 1972, p. 521).

Harris (1974) contended:

the most important aspect of any remedy for discrimination is the provision of firm financial exposure of persons who might otherwise discriminate. In the discrimination area, the possibility of a money penalty is more likely to prevent discrimination than any other remedy. . . . The increased concern of industrial firms to end racial discrimination when they face financial exposure assures me that this approach is valid, and I am sure such financial exposure will make the more national educational institutions willing to correct their misdeeds, both in training and hiring women (p. 25).

Many believe responsibility for change rests with individual institutions. Rumbarger (1973) concluded that

institutional reform and the elimination of discrimination cannot be accomplished simply through the imposition of external requirements by governmental agencies, although these may be, in many cases, a precondition for change. If change does not come from within the institution itself, and if proposed reforms are not supported by the internal structures and resources of the university community, remedies imposed by external agencies will be superficial and will fail to reach the roots of discrimination against women (p. 425).

Campbell (1970) spoke of changing the current investigation of HEW "from nuisance value to the recordkeepers to creative concern" (p. 61). The need for fundamental changes of attitude was expressed by many observers. Cross (1974) suggested that educators need to become as concerned with the pathways traversed as the ends reached. Many problems of women students—and men as well—could be solved if the educational setting would adapt more to individual lifestyles. Pifer (1971) concluded that "the real problem is not simply the prevention of discrimination against women but the promotion of their fuller participation in all aspects of higher education" (pp. 13-14). Improving conditions for women in higher education should benefit students of both sexes.

After considering all this, policy makers must be sure that burdens placed on the institutions relate to areas within their control. The graduate schools must deal with women who have already experienced many years of socialization, training, and other influences. Certainly the graduate schools must change their policies. This study will suggest areas that require attention. However, the whole burden cannot be placed on graduate schools; attention must be given to the determinants of preconditions.

Charges have been numerous that graduate schools discriminate against women students, in the sense that the inferior treatment of women is not justifiable by differences in merit between the sexes. One suggested area of differential treatment is the admissions process. Here persistent allegations are usually based either on data only tangentially relevant (for example, many more men than women receive doctorates) or anecdotal (for example, letters of reference for women frequently discuss the shapeliness of their figures).

Preliminary analysis of data only recently available on acceptance rates for individuals of both sexes who apply to graduate schools indicates that the acceptance rates for men and women are different. However, these statistics must be carefully analyzed before any firm conclusions can be drawn.

Would one expect institutions of higher education to discriminate against women in decisions about who to accept as students? It has been argued that in private, profit-seeking corporations discrimination is less than in regulated industries. When the choice is between profit maximization from hiring the most competent workers and the non-pecuniary benefits of selecting employees on bases other than merit, some evidence indicates that the profit motive dominates. In regulated firms, since profit rates cannot be altered much by increased productivity, the propensity to hire by subjective preference rather than productivity becomes stronger. Similar arguments relate to salary levels and promotions. A discussion of the relevant economic theory will help to determine whether universities can be expected to behave like regulated corporations.

RELEVANT ECONOMIC THEORY

Much economic theory assumes that the goal of a business enterprise is to maximize monetary profits. However, when considering wide-ranging business decisions, it is useful to generalize the profit-maximizing assumption to a utility-maximizing assumption. Becker (1957) has shown that, under the more general postulate, a person, deliberately and in full knowledge of the consequences for business profit or for personal wealth, will accept a lower salary or rate of return on invested capital in exchange for nonpecuniary income in the form of, say, working with pretty secretaries, nonforeigners, or whites. Becker's data indicate that blacks are discriminated against more frequently by monopolistic than by competitive enterprises. Presumably, the known sacrifice of pecuniary income due to the inefficiencies of discrimination is more than compensated for by the gain in nonpecuniary income from working with more desirable people.

Typically, monopolies are protected against the hazards of competition, not only by their ability to compete but also by state policy that does not permit competitors to enter monopolized markets (Alchian and Kessel 1962). Laws encourage monopolies in particular markets, such as public utilities. Monopolies so created are beholden to the state for their existence; their cardinal sin is to be too profitable. This constraint does not exist for firms in competitive markets, indicating differences between the business policies of competitive firms and monopolies. Even a firm that has successfully withstood the test of open competition without government protection may manifest the behavior of a protected monopoly. Thus, General Motors may acquire a large share of the market just as a protected monopoly does. If, in addition, its profits are large, it will fear that public policy or state action may be directed against it, just as against a state-created monopoly. Such a firm constrains its behavior much in the style of a monopoly whose profit position is protected but also watched by the state. If monopolies are too profitable, pressures are exerted to reduce profits by lowering prices. Only if monopolies can demonstrate to regulatory authorities that they are not sufficiently profitable are they permitted to raise prices.

If regulated monopolies can earn more than permissible pecuniary rates of return, inefficiency is a free good because the alternative is the same pecuniary income and no inefficiency. Therefore, this profit constraint leads to a divergence between private and economic costs. More properly, inefficiency is not involved at all, but rather efficient utility maximization through nonpecuniary gains. Clearly, one class of nonpecuniary income is indulging one's tastes in the kind of people one prefers. To take income in nonpecuniary form is consistent with maximizing utility. What is important is not difference in taste between monopolies and competitive firms but difference in the terms of trade of pecuniary for nonpecuniary income.

If wealth cannot be taken out of an organization in salaries or other forms of personal pecuniary property, the terms of trade between pecuniary wealth and nonpecuniary business-associated satisfactions turn against pecuniary wealth. In such a case, more organizational funds can be reinvested (which need not result in increased wealth) in ways that will enhance the manager's prestige or status in the community. Or more money can be spent for goods and services that enhance the manager's and employee's utility—luxurious offices, special services, and so forth—than would be spent if costs were coming out of personal wealth.

Employment policies also will reflect the maximization of utility. If two applicants are equally qualified but only one is white, native-born, Christian, and attractive, that person will get the job. And if the minority employee is willing to accept a lower wage in order to get the job, there will have to be a greater relative cut (or equilibrating difference) to enable him to get the job in a monopoly firm.

In the profit-seeking sector, if a pool of highly productive but underpaid (discriminated against) workers existed, possibly an entrepreneur could establish a competing firm, hire those discriminated against by increasing their pay, and make extraordinary profits. Apparently, this occurred in the advertising and publishing businesses recently when new firms established by women stressed hiring women. Both Freeman (1973) and Stiglitz (1973) have speculated about why this market mechanism has not worked more effectively in eliminating wage discrimination.

THE CASE OF HIGHER EDUCATION

Since institutions of higher learning are not run to maximize monetary returns, one might expect decision makers in higher education to maximize their total utility in ways analogous to decision makers in monopolistic industries. One manifestation of this behavior could be a decision to admit students most like the faculty and administration, that is, white men, so those running the institutions would feel comfortable with their student associates.

However, the analogy between institutions of higher education and private corporations whose profit potential is limited should not be carried too far. The question is whether or not institutions of higher education have a goal analogous to profits. One such goal might be maximum prestige for the institution. A measure of institutional reputation has been provided by the Cartter (1966) and Roose and Andersen (1970) ratings. An institution with a better reputation is generally more desirable in that it attracts brighter new faculty, better students, and more resources for research and other purposes. Enhanced prestige is a goal reached by expending resources of many kinds. If an institution seeks to maximize its reputation (Breneman 1970), it must trade off between utility maximization by discriminating in admissions and utility maximization by admitting those students most likely to enhance its reputation, particularly when some of the best applicants are women.

To hypothesize, say that (1) on the average, men and women make equally competent graduate students and (2) most men favor men as colleagues and students or in any professional relationship. In the most simplistic competitive model, all schools would admit the best applicants regardless of sex to maximize the quality of their student bodies. However, men-dominated faculties, favoring men over women students and seeking maximum institutional reputation, might effect a tradeoff between less qualified but more favored men and improving institutional reputation.

Certain classes of institutions might view this tradeoff between "desirable" students and institutional reputation differently. Some might think that, potentially, any discrimination could cause significant reductions in institutional quality or that, by admitting the most capable students, institutional reputation could be increased. Others might think that the potential for improving quality is so small that the cost of discriminating in admissions is also small. This view might predominate at institutions with either top reputations or exceedingly low status.

If women were systematically discriminated against, an ambitious poor-quality institution could explicitly seek top-quality women students who would not be accepted by the top institutions to improve its average student quality, and hence, its reputation. The top institutions might have such a glut of superior applications that they could discriminate and still maintain high student quality. However, the middle-quality institutions with fewer high-quality men applicants might favor women.

Moreover, the poorest graduate schools might be worried less about quality than survival. These schools would need students to fill classes and to assure continued employment to faculty. If these poor schools had a choice of men or women students, they would probably choose men even if the women had better credentials. However, if the better schools took most of the qualified men, the poorer institutions would be more likely to have the women they accept actually enroll, since the men would also have been accepted at better schools. Poor schools in competition with better schools that favor men probably have difficulty ignoring women.

To reiterate, if faculties and administrations dominated by men prefer men as colleagues and students but seek to maximize institutional reputation, the most elite institutions would be among the most discriminatory. Their applicant pool is so large that quality and reputation could be maintained while they select primarily from among men. It is more difficult to predict the extent of discrimination at the lowest-quality institutions. On the one hand, the need to survive with a limited applicant pool would probably result in a weaker tendency to favor men. On the other hand, the desire to improve the institutional reputation might be reduced by a sense of futility. If decision makers believe that no matter which admissions policy is adopted, the chances of improving reputation are minimal, they will seek other goals, such as compatible colleagues.

Schools in the middle of the prestige hierarchy would probably discriminate less against women applicants. These institutions aspire to better reputations and have some reasonable chance of reaching their goal. In the tradeoff between the probability of improving reputation by accepting the best applicants, regardless of sex, and the benefit from working with men, these schools would be more likely to favor reputation. They are close enough to the top that their decision makers view as real the possibility of reaching the higher echelon. Middle-level schools with a realistic chance of moving up will trade off their desire for men students most easily to improve their reputation. This group does not have a large enough pool of excellent men applicants to discriminate and improve reputation.

If men at poor schools are unwilling to seek women students, a few institutions exclusively for women might develop graduate schools, although this is a poor analogy to the new business firms established by women. Establishing a new (and accredited) graduate school is more difficult than establishing a new advertising agency. Universities might collude to inhibit growth of new institutions, which would satisfy faculties dominated by men and reduce later competition in the labor market. An established professor might prefer competition from less competent men than from more competent women.

In certain cases, the best schools might discriminate less. Since these institutions are eager to maintain top-quality students, in times of reduced applications, they might look more seriously at applications from women. During periods of low demand for admissions, the best schools would have to go "deeper into the barrel" if they sought only men students.

At least part of the contributions of students to a school's reputation comes after graduation. In a production company, the outcomes are separate from the inputs; one does not know whether a bicycle has been produced by a black, a white, a man, or a woman. However, the product of the graduate school cannot be disassociated from the sex of the student input: When a woman graduate applies for a job, she is still a woman. Unless the employment opportunities do not depend on sex (and they probably do), a "competitive" school might not benefit as much from training women, since even the best women will get inferior jobs.

DATA ON ACCEPTANCE RATES

In a survey of the deans of doctoral-granting institutions, 84 schools provided data on applications and acceptances by sex. These 84 are representative of the total 240 doctoral-granting institutions in terms of institutional quality, size, and region. (See Appendix D for a list of participating institutions.) Over two-thirds of the 240 institutions returned completed questionnaires, and one-half of these (that is, 85) provide the data about admissions rates by sex. There is no reason to assume that the institutions that provided data were more or less discriminatory than those that did not. These data deal with individuals admitted for fall 1972. Cost and data availability problems precluded collecting statistics on a department-by-department basis. However, in some later analyses, different field mixes of graduates of various institutions were controlled for.

Table 2.1 shows acceptance/application rates of schools classified by Roose-Andersen (1970). For almost all groups, women are favored in admissions (assume for the moment equal abilities). However, in the top-ranked schools, more applications from men are accepted. In the next two categories, women are favored slightly (statistically insignificant). Women are most favored among the schools in the middle Roose-Andersen range. Women are also selected in greater proportion than men at the poorest schools, but the favoritism here is less than at the schools rated directly above the poorest.

TABLE 2.1

Sex Favoritism in Doctoral-Granting Institutions of Differing Quality

Institution (Roose-Andersen Rating)	Acceptance/Application		Coefficient of Favoritism*
	Men	Women	
4+	.314	.295	6.05
3.99 – 3.50	.298	.308	-3.36
3.49 – 3.00	.394	.409	-3.81
2.99 – 2.50	.504	.572	-13.49
2.49 – 2.00	.565	.645	-14.16
1.99 – 1.50	.485	.524	-8.04
1.49 – 1.00	.717	.789	-10.04
Not rated	.626	.683	-9.11

*The difference between the acceptance/application rates for men and women, divided by the rate for men times 100. A negative coefficient indicates women are favored.

Source: Compiled by the author.

TABLE 2.2

Scores on Graduate Record Examination Specialty Tests, by Sex

	Institution (Roose-Andersen Rating)							
Field	4.0 - 3.496	3.495 - 2.996	2.995 - 2.496	2.495 - 1.996	1.995 - 1.496	1.495 - 0.996	0.996	Not rated
Biology								
Men	690.86	667.74	638.30	628.60	620.18	606.70	571.82	622.89
Women	679.82	657.85	635.48	625.80	614.15	600.44	576.43	612.89
Chemistry								
Men	695.00	664.07	648.86	623.21	615.11	645.20	580.06	616.45
Women	647.31	633.94	628.92	618.27	625.52	651.78	584.00	630.90
Economics								
Men	673.15	638.69	619.96	598.48	586.58	621.99	505.00	579.52
Women	629.89	607.27	588.76	572.19	563.84	576.45	0.0	551.07
Education								
Men	499.21	494.65	486.42	493.71	485.57	460.98	490.00	464.64
Women	480.99	479.78	473.71	481.17	472.96	454.94	473.28	449.17
Engineering								
Men	649.35	631.47	628.65	603.16	607.04	627.69	595.00	583.58
Women	601.98	614.79	619.28	597.66	586.92	580.00	0.0	592.74
French								
Men	598.70	573.17	562.68	546.79	532.62	529.26	0.0	531.37
Women	574.90	557.52	544.20	535.78	536.86	515.07	555.83	528.11
Geography								
Men	513.67	504.52	506.06	485.67	484.95	462.02	0.0	476.79
Women	466.75	465.57	438.68	436.86	453.91	396.11	0.0	440.41
Geology								
Men	632.21	602.01	596.74	584.09	575.46	581.58	552.00	584.55
Women	612.00	591.68	584.49	576.95	580.86	576.44	610.00	569.30
German								
Men	570.30	556.63	519.42	509.29	504.20	499.55	0.0	511.54
Women	578.33	541.37	532.04	523.17	522.49	513.21	460.00	519.46

		1	2	3	4	5	6	7	8
History	Men	590.68	578.34	564.62	554.40	545.40	533.76	516.71	536.27
	Women	559.64	543.62	536.54	529.05	525.58	512.81	507.61	515.48
Literature	Men	615.55	599.34	582.73	572.63	561.69	554.87	535.36	558.92
	Women	595.48	581.46	566.25	558.94	550.47	534.17	515.10	541.60
Mathematics	Men	801.74	758.10	721.45	697.91	673.56	748.38	671.80	668.81
	Women	695.60	677.18	651.90	629.49	610.28	618.00	642.00	607.61
Music	Men	572.92	546.15	534.82	515.55	521.99	488.97	0.0	507.07
	Women	540.65	512.96	495.36	477.98	481.70	460.28	0.0	481.11
Philosophy	Men	715.79	696.15	693.49	678.22	656.88	654.59	585.30	652.63
	Women	662.05	661.14	626.76	630.35	635.75	617.02	720.00	627.69
Physics	Men	726.03	690.83	646.73	646.67	629.38	684.26	556.56	638.97
	Women	649.54	658.49	625.60	600.98	616.32	693.11	415.00	631.20
Political Science	Men	539.76	523.19	511.66	503.60	494.19	487.69	469.61	488.78
	Women	503.57	497.42	479.12	472.80	466.55	466.94	445.00	448.87
Psychology	Men	579.79	574.32	559.87	554.30	549.95	549.23	539.79	546.12
	Women	560.70	559.24	548.19	542.10	537.54	534.19	547.13	533.95
Sociology	Men	577.69	557.89	543.00	516.12	497.54	482.42	434.29	498.34
	Women	528.70	522.27	508.30	484.90	472.09	453.97	483.59	444.58
Spanish	Men	604.52	596.19	597.10	577.99	564.11	529.21	615.69	555.55
	Women	580.36	557.12	555.14	544.47	526.36	510.56	541.93	537.65

Note: Data are from a tape provided by the Educational Testing Service and cover all doctorate-granting institutions. The figures in the table are mean scores of all those who took the particular test in 1971-72 and 1972-73 and who had their scores sent in 1972-73 to institutions falling in the specified ranges of Roosevelt-Andersen ratings. The file included the most recent eight institutions to which the student had his scores sent. Hence, one student's scores could appear in the average score of up to eight institutions.

The best schools seem able to maintain their quality while
favoring men. The next group, presumably those with aspirations of
moving to the top, admit the greatest share of women applicants. In
world without discrimination, these women might have been accepted
by the best schools. Finally, the lowest-quality schools do favor
women, although not to the extent of those nearer the top in quality.
This favoritism might reflect a desire to maintain enrollments, given
the knowledge that the more attractive schools are more likely to
accept men.

Only 25 (29 percent) of the 84 doctoral-granting institutions
admitted a higher proportion of men than women applicants, a percentage
perhaps disarming to those who claim that graduate schools discriminate
in admissions. However, some proponents of this notion counter by
stating that women applicants are, on the average, superior to men,
the theory being that women are so discouraged from postbaccalaureate
training that only the best persevere. The evidence most often cited to
support this view is Harmon (1965), who showed that the high school
grade point averages of women doctoral recipients are higher than those
of men recipients. However, these data are quite irrelevant for acceptance ratios.

Needed here are data on the relative qualities of men and women
applicants, rather than graduates. Table 2.2 presents data on all
doctorate-granting institutions for 1971-72 and 1972-73. The average
graduate record examination (GRE) scores of men and women who apply
to each doctoral-granting institution show that men score higher than
women (statistically significant) on the quantitative test, while women
score somewhat higher than men (not statistically significant) on the
verbal test. These scores are not surprising to many, given the nature
of high school and college training for men and women. The general
assumption is that men are encouraged to take more quantitative subjects. Data by sex for scores on the GRE specialty tests are presented
in Table 2.2.

For applicants to institutions at each quality level, men score
slightly higher than women in virtually every specialty test. This
discrepancy prevails in the "feminine" fields of literature, music, and
education as well as in the "masculine" fields of economics, engineering, and mathematics. Statistical tests of the differences in means
reveal that these sex differences are not statistically significant. However, at the time of application, women are not demonstrably superior
to men, if GRE is an index of student ability.

It has been argued that to be admitted to the best graduate
schools, women must graduate from better undergraduate institutions,
ceteris paribus. Although data on baccalaureate origins of applicants
to graduate schools were not readily available, Table 2.3 provides data
on the undergraduate institutions of 1972 Ph.D. recipients. These
data probably reflect patterns of acceptances for at least the top

TABLE 2.3

Ratings of Undergraduate Institutions of 1972 Doctoral Recipients

Graduate Institution (Roose-Andersen Rating)	Cartter Category of Undergraduate Institution*									
	1	2	6	3	7	4	8	5	9	10
Men										
4.0 - 3.496	20.50	34.13	40.69	48.52	56.37	64.31	69.19	74.99	78.39	79.43
3.495 - 2.996	7.21	28.10	32.19	39.61	48.88	57.90	63.53	71.79	78.76	80.96
2.995 - 2.496	3.86	13.16	16.05	33.20	45.24	55.22	61.82	71.83	81.71	84.31
2.495 - 1.996	3.38	9.86	12.02	25.40	35.19	51.60	59.42	70.05	83.26	86.40
1.995 - 1.496	2.06	6.57	7.67	14.81	23.22	45.69	53.47	67.48	83.58	87.52
1.495 - 0.996	7.58	13.99	15.97	21.75	29.00	42.24	47.54	66.53	82.79	87.04
Under 0.996	0.0	1.68	2.52	15.13	32.78	54.63	60.51	70.59	79.83	91.59
Not rated	2.96	9.53	11.55	19.66	31.29	42.04	51.35	67.83	81.85	86.83
Women										
4.0 - 3.496	14.20	27.55	47.58	55.61	65.34	70.95	75.42	79.89	85.86	87.49
3.495 - 2.996	3.90	24.44	36.69	44.99	56.20	63.26	69.19	75.36	83.11	85.95
2.995 - 2.496	3.42	13.68	22.42	38.63	51.42	59.21	66.05	73.14	84.16	88.09
2.495 - 1.996	2.32	10.61	16.10	33.30	44.15	56.04	64.27	71.10	84.94	90.0
1.995 - 1.496	2.13	8.31	13.31	20.08	27.44	48.93	56.07	68.14	84.99	90.29
1.495 - 0.996	1.75	8.75	13.81	18.87	25.68	41.63	48.83	65.37	85.02	93.58
Under 0.996	0.0	2.33	13.96	20.94	32.57	53.50	69.78	76.76	93.04	95.37
Not rated	2.07	10.21	15.20	24.56	36.23	45.67	53.11	68.38	82.42	88.94

Note: Table shows cumulative percentage of Ph.D. recipients from institutions of each quality level coming from successive levels of undergraduate institutions.

*Unpublished ratings by A. M. Cartter, 1974. Categories 1 through 5 are graduate institutions, 6 through 10 undergraduate institutions. Order reflects comparisons of graduate and undergraduate institutions; hence, category 6 follows 1 and 2.

graduate schools; since few men or women from the poorest undergraduate institutions are accepted by the best graduate schools; those who are accepted are probably so exceptional that they receive the doctorate and, hence, are reflected in the data on graduates.

Twenty percent of men who received a Ph.D. in 1972 from schools with Roose-Andersen ratings above 3.5 came from undergraduate institutions rated by Cartter (1966) as among those of highest quality. Cartter's categories provide rankings of undergraduate institutions that parallel the graduate rankings. Only 14 percent of women with doctorates from the best schools came from the top undergraduate category. It appears that more women than men could get doctorates from the best graduate schools if they attended a less than top undergraduate institution. A look at the best three categories of undergraduate institutions (1, 2, and 6) shows that more women than men in the top Roose-Andersen category came from these institutions. Since category 6 includes the most elite women's colleges (the "seven sisters"), one can argue that women graduating from the best doctoral-granting institutions did come from undergraduate institutions of higher prestige.

REGRESSION ANALYSIS OF INSTITUTIONAL DIFFERENCES

After observing acceptance rates, which generally favor women when means for groups of institutions of different quality are considered, differences among individual graduate institutions were explained by regression analysis. The general procedure was to explain differences in the acceptance rates for men applicants, then explain acceptance rates for women applicants separately. The objective was to see whether certain explanatory variables had different effects on the decisions to accept men and women. It was then possible to apply to women the weights used for men to see whether the acceptance rates for women would differ if the criteria for men were applied.

In general, three categories of variables were used to explain acceptance rates for applicants of a particular sex. The first set dealt with the characteristics of the applicants. The most important student-related variable in this category was the average GRE score of all applicants to a particular institution. These scores were available separately for applicants of each sex. Data on both the GRE quantitative and verbal tests were available, as well as mean scores on the specialty tests. Apparently, the verbal score explains slightly more of the institution-by-institution differences in acceptance rates for both men and women than the quantitative score. Hence, verbal scores were used for most of the tests here. In addition to the mean score of applicants, the variance among applicants was a significant determinant of acceptance rates. Hence, the standard deviation of the mean scores was included for members of each sex who applied to a school.

The second important student-related variable was the number of applications by each student. Since institutions are the units of observation in this analysis, this variable was measured by the number of applicants to each institution. As expected, the larger the number of applicants of a particular sex to a particular institution, the lower the percentage of applicants of that sex accepted, ceteris paribus. Another student-related variable was the quality of undergraduate institutions attended by applicants. Although specific data were unavailable, available information on the quality of institutions attended by doctoral recipients sufficed. For the regressions, a variable measuring the proportion of recent doctoral recipients who attended the most elite undergraduate institutions was developed, on the assumption that the flow patterns of doctoral recipients from undergraduate to graduate institutions reflected flow patterns of all applicants. Finally, the proportion of applicants accepted who actually matriculated at particular institutions was inserted as a variable, the argument being that schools with a lower show-up rate might accept a higher proportion of applicants. Neither of these two variables appeared significant in explaining institutional differences in acceptance rates, so they are not included below.

Do women tend to apply to institutions where other women have been successful in the past? If this were the case, institutions that receive applications from women and have had good prior experiences might favor women. However, differences among graduate schools in the number of women who apply were not explained by the percentage of Ph.D.'s awarded to women or the percentage of women accepted from among those who applied. Apparently, women do not consider past history of women at an institution an important factor in their application decisions.

The second set of variables used to explain acceptance rates was the institution's experiences with earlier students. A number of variables representing average characteristics of recent doctoral recipients were inserted in the regressions to explain acceptance rates on the assumption that the decision would be made with full consideration of the traits of earlier graduates. The problem here was that the data only pertained to those who received doctorates and might be quite different if they included those who dropped out before receiving the Ph.D. In any case, variables such as the proportion of recipients who were married at the time they received the doctorate, the time between the bachelor's and doctoral degrees, and the proportion of Ph.D. recipients who are women were included in the regressions.

The nature of the institutions themselves suggested a third set of variables that might explain acceptance rates, the most important being the size of first-year graduate school enrollment. Everything else being constant, institutions with larger classes would tend to accept a higher proportion of applicants. The Roose-Andersen rating (1970) of an institution, considered significant, was positively correlated with both GRE scores and number of applicants, as were Astin's estimates (1971) of institutional selectivity.

Another variable suggested in some regressions was public or private institutional control. Although public institutions are more accountable, the data did not confirm that they are less likely to discriminate.

Does the financial condition of the university influence acceptance patterns? On the one hand, affluence (measured by revenue per student) might affect acceptance rates, since less affluent institutions would feel compelled to accept a larger share of those applying to assure a revenue inflow. On the other hand, aid per student was inserted in the regressions to see whether schools that traditionally provided more student financial aid would have lower acceptance rates because they sought to assure that more of those who were accepted could be supported financially. Tuition also was inserted in some regressions as a variable that might affect acceptance rates, the hypothesis being that schools with higher tuition might accept more students who would then become valuable revenue producers.

Another variable, the number of Ph.D.'s awarded in the natural sciences, was used to see whether overall graduate acceptance rates were affected by the field mix of an institution. (Initially, it was hypothesized that institutions awarding a larger proportion of doctorates in the natural sciences would be less likely to accept women. However, since many institutions were awarding Ph.D.'s exclusively either in the natural sciences or in the arts and humanities, the proportional variable was dropped.)

Another variable was the proportion of women faculty, the question being whether institutions with more women faculty were influenced by these women to accept more women students.

Differences in acceptance rates among institutions can be explained primarily by three variables: the number of applicants, the total number of students enrolled in first-year graduate study, and the mean and standard deviation of the GRE scores of applicants.

Table 2.4 reveals three strong relationships that remain unaltered by other explanatory variables. First, the larger the number of applicants of a particular sex, the lower the percentage of applicants of that sex accepted. The logic of this negative sign on the number of applicants is obvious: controlling for student quality as measured by GRE and for class size as measured by total enrollment, one would expect that the more who apply, the fewer accepted.

Second, the larger the class size or ultimate total enrollment in the first year, the higher the acceptance rate. This also appears logical since, controlling for the number and quality of applicants, one would expect that, where class size is larger, a greater proportion of applicants would be accepted.

The third relationship, a negative relationship between the average GRE scores of applicants and the proportion of applicants accepted, is

TABLE 2.4

Regressions to Explain Acceptance Rates at Institutions Grouped by Selectivity

	Institution							
	Total		Roose-Andersen Rating > 2.5		Roose-Andersen Rating < 2.5		Unranked	
	Men	Women	Men	Women	Men	Women	Men	Women
Regression								
GRE verbal	-.0027	-.00179	-.00313	-.00365	-.00149·	-.00110	-.00349	-.00097[a]
Number of applicants	-.00005	-.00013	-.00002	-.00003[a]	-.00012	-.00019	-.00005	-.00030[a]
Total enrollment	.00011	.00011	.00005[a]	.00004[a]	.00022	.00011[a]	.00013	.00021[a]
Constant	1.9624	1.6018	2.13425	2.5069	1.37572	1.30225	2.36726	1.2083
R^2	.5725	.3467	.81091	.73861	.48215	.35312	.60481	.16542
Observations	80	80	19	19	29	29	32	32
Means								
GRE verbal	514	527	542	561	510	518	501	514
Number of applicants	2030	872	4269	1715	1699	872	1000	372
Total enrollment	709		1223		698		414	
Acceptances/applications	.5556	.6184	.4204	.4605	.5704	.6472	.6223	.6860
Coefficient of favoritism	-11.30		-9.53		-13.46		-10.24	
Predicted acceptances/applications for women[b]	.5739		.4053		.6552		.6095	

[a]F < 2.0.
[b]Obtained by plugging mean values of independent variables for women into estimated equation for men.

surprising. Most explanations for this negative sign disappear since class size and number of applicants are already controlled for. Schools with the best applicant pool appear to select a relatively small proportion of their good applicants. The more elite institutions receive a larger number of applications; higher GRE scores are evident in these applications, although the variance in the mean GRE is highest at the best schools. Perhaps the show-up rate for those accepted is higher at the better schools (more applicants really want to go there; the school is not just a safety valve), and so a desired class can be obtained by accepting fewer students, given the quality and number of applicants and class size (whereas nonelite schools must overaccept to assure class size).

Berelson (1960) pointed out that better schools have a better chance to select better students; they have more applicants and, generally, first choice among them. But at the same time, precisely because they are the national graduate schools, they register fewer of those admitted:

	Percentage of Applicants Admitted	Percentage of Applicants Admitted Who Register
Top 12 universities	48	53
Remaining universities	71	72

The better students apply to several better schools, are admitted to a few, then register at one. The lesser institutions are more regionally based: They admit large proportions of their applicants to have graduate students, and large proportions of these applicants actually register, since they have applied to only the admitting institution or perhaps one other. Thus, multiple applications are a problem only at the top of the pyramid; as more students apply for graduate study, the rich will get richer in the sense that the top universities will have even more of the top talent to select from (p. 111).

In explaining the proportion of applicants accepted, a positive coefficient on average GRE scores of applicants would be expected. In the most direct sense, better-quality applicants should be accepted more frequently. Moreover, schools that get better applicants are probably willing to enroll more of them. Better students may want assurance of admission to the best quality institutions and, for safety, apply to more schools to be certain of admission to at least one good school. These students have a higher no-show probability at any one school for a given probability of acceptance. Schools with better applicants probably have fewer of those accepted show up and, hence, must accept a higher proportion of applicants to reach a target enrollment. All these reasons point to a positive coefficient. The only argument for a negative coefficient is that better schools get more applicants and schools with more applicants accept fewer students. One would expect better applicants to apply to schools where more students apply, so any one school might accept fewer of these better applicants. However, the number of applicants was controlled for in the regression.

Two other explanations help to clarify the relationship between average GRE scores and acceptance rates. First, institutions with student applicants who have, on average, a higher mean GRE might also have a higher variance in applicant quality. When the variance is considered with the mean GRE scores of applicants, the results might be reversed. Table 2.5 replicates Table 2.4 with an additional variable, the product of the mean GRE scores of applicants and the mean standard deviation of the mean GRE. The coefficient on this product variable tells whether or not the variance of the GRE score of applicants affects the relationship between the mean score and the dependent variable.* Apparently, the variance has virtually no impact on the relationship for men. However, in the regressions to explain acceptance rates of women, the product term is significant and positive, reducing the negative effect of average GRE score in the acceptance rate. When the variance is added to the regression for women, the R^2 increases substantially.

The second factor that might alter the relationship between average GRE scores of applicants and acceptance rates is that the GRE score as a requirement for admission to graduate school is not similar across institutions. Indeed 48 percent of the schools in this sample indicated in their catalogs that the GRE or other entrance examination requirement varied by department (that is, some departments, but not all, required the GRE, while some departments required another test instead of the GRE). This finding varied according to the Roose-Andersen rating of the schools. In the highest-ranked schools, whether or not the GRE was required varied more across departments than in the lower-ranked or unranked schools. In many cases the GRE was suggested, or an indication was given that good GRE scores might improve acceptance chances, or the GRE was required only for students with less than superior standing in some other admissions requirement. The implication is that the average of the GRE scores of all students who had their scores sent to a particular school is not necessarily a consistent indicator of the quality of all applicants.

For 61 of the 85 schools used in the regressions, data were available on the departmental requirement of the GRE aptitude tests for 15 representative fields (Graduate Record Examination Board, 1973). Each department indicating "required" received a value of 4, "recommended" a value of 3, "required under certain circumstances" a value of 2, and "not required" a value of 1. An institutional mean was obtained by weighting the value assigned to a department by the number of Ph.D.'s awarded in 1972. The institutional weighted means

---

*With the interaction term in the equation, $Acc/App = a + bGRE + cGRE(SD)$, $d(Acc/App)/dGRE = b + c(SD)$. If $b < 0$ and $c > 0$, then the total effect of GRE is less than when the interaction term is omitted.

were then correlated with the means and standard deviations of the average GRE scores of those who applied to each institution. These correlations are presented below:

GRE verbal	Mean M	.3500
GRE verbal	SD M	.1431
GRE verbal	Mean F	.2319
GRE verbal	SD F	.0512
GRE quantitative	Mean M	.2978
GRE quantitative	SD M	-.0470
GRE quantitative	Mean F	.1366
GRE quantitative	SD F	-.1251

The correlation is positive between the average aptitude test scores of individuals applying to an institution and the degree to which these tests are required by that institution. Where scores are high, all students are more likely to have been required to take the test. This seems reasonable, because institutions where the test was less than required were likely to receive scores from less qualified students. A negative correlation between GRE scores and acceptance rates, therefore, implies a negative correlation between the extent to which GRE scores are required and the admissions rate. That is, schools that require GRE scores are likely to admit a lower proportion of applicants. To look at this the other way, schools relying more on requirements other than the GRE are more likely to have higher acceptance rates.

Since the correlations between the mean score of applicants and the degree to which these tests are required are higher for men than women, the negative coefficient on GRE in explaining acceptance rates should be larger for men than women, assuming that the regression coefficient is really standing for the degree to which these tests are required. This was indeed the case, except among the most highly rated institutions (see Table 2.4). The implication is that, except at the best schools, if more subjective criteria are given greater weight in the admissions decision, men tend to be accepted more readily than women. The GRE score, by bringing more objective evidence into the decision-making process, tends to lessen the favoring of men.

In Table 2.4, columns 1 and 2 indicate that over 50 percent of the variance in acceptance rates of men applicants in the 85 schools can be explained by the three variables of average GRE scores, number of applicants, and total first-year graduate enrollment. A third of the variance in the acceptance rates of women applicants can be explained by the same model. The other columns show results of the same regression analysis performed on three subgroups: schools with Roose-Andersen quality ratings equal to or more than 2.5, those with ratings below 2.5, and those with no Roose-Andersen rating. This three-part classification breaks the schools roughly into quality thirds, with

TABLE 2.5

Regressions to Explain Acceptance Rates with the Variance of Average GRE Scores Included

	Institution							
	Total		Roose-Andersen Rating 2.5		Roose-Andersen Rating 2.5		Unranked	
	Men	Women	Men	Women	Men	Women	Men	Women
Regression								
GRE verbal	-.00269	-.00452	-.00401	-.00416	0*	-.00201*	-.00304	-.00539
Number of applicants	-.00005	-.00014	-.00003	0*	-.00012	-.00019	-.00006	-.00043
Total enrollment	.00011	.00010	-.00008	0*	.00023	0	.00013	.00031
GRE verbal times standard deviation	-	-.00002	.00001	0*	0*	0*	0*	.00002
Constant	1.9624	2.1088	2.0474	2.4730	1.2751	1.2767	2.4341	2.2630
R^2	.5725	.4906	.8454	.7427	.4913	.3697	.6189	.5233
Observations	80	80	19	19	29	29	32	32
Means								
GRE verbal	514	527	542	561	510	518	501	514
Number of applicants	2030	872	4269	1715	1699	872	1000	372
Total enrollment	708		1223		698		414	
Standard deviation of GRE	119	115	126	121	117	114	119	111
GRE standard deviation	61397	61029	68108	67581	59276	60041	59335	58035
Acceptances/admissions	.5556	.6184	.4204	.4605	.5704	.6472	.6223	.6860
Predicted acceptances/admissions for women		.5791		.5199		1.331		.903

*F < 2.0

the unranked schools having lower quality than any schools with a rating. (All schools awarding at least 100 doctorates in two or more disciplines in the 10 years preceding the Roose-Andersen ratings were ranked. Hence, the unranked schools are either small or new. Few new or small doctorate-granting institutions are of high quality, although there are a few exceptions.)

More than 80 percent of the variance of acceptance rates for men in the most elite institutions and over 73 percent of the variance for women can be explained by this analysis. Note that the three-way breakdown in Table 2.4 is more aggregated than the breakdown in Table 2.1; hence, some patterns differ between tables (for a list of the schools whose data are analyzed, see Appendix B). The R^2 for men falls to below 0.5 in the lower-ranked schools but is over 0.6 in the unranked institutions. However, for women the R^2 in the lower-ranked institutions falls to 0.35 and to 0.17 in the unranked institutions. That is, the explainable portion of difference in acceptance rates for women declines much more quickly in the move to the low and unranked schools. Apparently, in the highest quality institutions the decision to accept men and women involves consideration of the same variables. In lower-quality institutions, these variables are less pertinent to women. Either other variables come into play or acceptance of women is more a random process.

Table 2.4 also provides data on the average acceptance rates for applicants of each sex for three subgroups of institutions and for all institutions combined. As expected, the proportion of applicants accepted increases as the quality of the group decreases. In each subgroup of institutions, a higher proportion of women than men applicants is accepted. These data are consistent with those in Table 2.1, which also reveal generally higher acceptance rates for women. Once again, it is the middle-quality schools that show the largest degree of favoritism toward women.

The regression coefficients in Table 2.4 indicate that the impact of the three explanatory variables is different when explaining the acceptance rates for men and women. What would the acceptance rates for women be if the effect of GRE scores of applicants, the number of applicants, and the total enrollment were the same for both sexes? To answer this question, the mean values of the three variables for women applicants were inserted in the regression equation for men, a procedure that yields a predicted acceptance rate for women if standards for men are applied (Astin and Bayer 1972).

If the standards for men had been applied to women for all graduate schools, the estimated proportion of women accepted would still have been higher than the observed proportion of men but would have been lower than the observed acceptance rate for women. The predicted acceptance rates for women in the elite and unranked institutions are lower than the actual rates for men, implying that, in these institutions, women are better off in terms of acceptance than they would be if judged by masculine standards. Indeed, there seems to be some explicit discrimination in favor of women.

In schools rated below 2.5, women would have higher predicted acceptance rates (compared with actual rates) if they were judged by masculine criteria. Only in this group does some favoritism toward men appear. An alternative approach was to plug the male means into the female coefficients to find the proportion of men who would have been accepted if these decisions were based on the criteria for women. When this was used, in virtually every case, the predicted acceptance rate for men was lower than the actual rate. The results remained consistent.

Although the schools rated below 2.5 favor women to the greatest degree, application of male weights would have led to even greater acceptance of women. This approach of applying mean values of one sex to weights obtained from estimation of an equation for the other sex assumes that the same factors determine success for men and women. However, unless the factors that predict success for men and women are known, one cannot a priori advocate equal standards. The question here is merely: What would the results have been, given equal treatment?—with no intent to advocate this policy, since individual differences do exist between and within the sexes.

Table 2.5 alters the regression estimates of Table 2.4 by inserting an additional variable, the average GRE score on the verbal test of applicants times the variance of the GRE scores of applicants at a particular school. The results do not differ when the standard deviation is inserted alone, rather than as a cross-product term. The addition of the product term alters the results in several ways: The power of the equation explaining differences in acceptance rates for men does not increase at all. However, the explanatory power of the model for acceptance rates for women rises significantly from 0.347 to 0.491.

Among the elite institutions, those with Roose-Andersen ratings equal to or greater than 2.5, it is now possible to explain almost 85 percent of the difference in acceptance rates for men and almost 75 percent of the variance for women. However, in the regression for women, the only variable with a significant coefficient is still the average GRE score (verbal) of applicants. The R^2 for the equation for women in the unranked institutions increases from 0. 65 to 0.523 with the addition of the product term. In this group, the variance in quality of applicants is important in admissions decisions. Given any mean level of applicant quality, a wider dispersion in individual scores implies a greater acceptance rate; that is, probably more of the higher-scoring applicants are accepted. In the low-rated group of schools, the GRE scores and the product term are insignificant, with only the number of applicants and the total enrollment significant for women.

Finally, the results obtained by applying the female means to the male weights from Table 2.4 change somewhat when the regressions in

Table 2.5 are used. For the total regression, the predicted value of the acceptance rate for women using coefficients from the regression for men falls to 0.579 from the actual rate of 0.618, only insignificantly higher than the predicted value from Table 2.4. The predicted acceptance rate for women using male coefficients and female means for the elite schools is 0.520 (rather than 0.420 from the regression not using the standard deviation), compared with the actual acceptance rate for women of 0.461 and for men of 0.420. Women would do better at the elite schools if men's criteria were applied to them. However, in the nonelite and unranked schools, the predicted acceptance rates for women are less meaningful: an acceptance rate in the nonelite schools of over 1.0 and in the unranked schools of 0.9. Hence, this methodology appears to fall apart once the standard deviation is included to explain acceptance rates.

Alternative specifications also were tested substituting the GRE scores in the quantitative test for the verbal test and including both the GRE quantitative and verbal in the same regression with the two corresponding product terms, including the standard deviation. The R^2, when the quantitative scores and cross-product term were substituted, fell from 0.5725 to 0.4404 for men and from 0.4906 to 0.3010 for women. When both the verbal and quantitative scores were used at the same time, the R^2 for men rose to 0.5842 and for women to 0.5549. The pattern of the other variable did not change significantly. Therefore, further analysis used GRE verbal alone.

Table 2.6 extends the analysis for the whole group of schools by including, in two separate sets of regressions, the additional variables that might affect acceptance rates. With all additional variables, the proportion of variance in acceptance rates for men explained rises from the 0.573 reported in Table 2.5 to 0.590. In other words, the additional variables add virtually nothing to the explanatory power of the model for men. However, the additional variables increase the R^2 in the equation for women from 0.491 to 0.601. Hence, the suggested additional variables do have some effect on decisions about accepting women. The four variables used in Table 2.5 have the same statistical significance even when additional variables are added.

Three additional variables appear significant in explaining acceptance rates: the number of Ph.D.'s awarded in a recent year in the natural sciences, the percentage of recent women graduates who are married, and the percentage of women faculty. In the equations for both men and women, the larger the number of Ph.D.'s in the natural sciences, ceteris paribus, the lower the acceptance rate. Although this negative coefficient does not differ significantly from zero in the regression for men, it is statistically significant and negative in the regression for women, with a magnitude over three times as great as the coefficient in the male regression. Apparently, institutions similar in size, student quality, and so forth are less likely to admit women if a larger proportion of their graduate training is in the

TABLE 2.6

Full Model to Explain Acceptance Rates for All Schools Combined

	Regression 1		Regression 2	
	Men	Women	Men	Women
GRE verbal	-.00288	-.00459	-.00312	-.00426
Verbal standard deviation	0^a	.00002	0^a	.00002
Number of applicants	-.00004	-.0001	-.00005	-.00011
Total enrollment	.00011	.0001	.0001	.0001
RA (dummy)[b]	.01297[a]	-.00015[a]	-.01458[a]	.01021[a]
Number natural science Ph.D.'s	-.00018[a]	-.00064	.00002[a]	-.00041
Percent married	-.00063[a]	-.00119	-.00065[a]	-.00092
Percent women Ph.D.'s	.1269[a]	.03122[a]	.13532[a]	.1207[a]
Percent women faculty			.20791[a]	.8442
Affluence code			.00095[a]	.01375[a]
Control			.02469[a]	.01518[a]
Constant	2.0975	2.0997	2.1390	1.8054
R^2	.5796	.5418	.5896	.6008
Observations	80	80	76	76

[a]$F < 2.0$.
[b]RA (dummy) variable equals 1 if the school's Roose-Andersen rating is equal to or greater than 2.5, and 0 otherwise.

natural sciences. Since these fields historically have been dominated by men, this result is not surprising. These data do not allow a comparison of acceptance rates specifically in the natural science fields, particularly while controlling for the abilities of the men and women applying for admission to these particular programs. However, this negative relationship between acceptance rates for women and the number of doctorates awarded in the natural sciences could be due to the lower acceptance rates for women applying for admission to natural science programs.

The variable indicating the percentage of women faculty appears to be positive in the regressions for both men and women. However, the coefficient in the regression for men is not significantly different from zero (according to the t-test). The positive coefficient on this variable is statistically significant in the regression for women with a magnitude four times greater than that in the regression for men. This result is logical, since it implies that acceptance rates for women will be significantly higher when a larger proportion of women are already on the faculty. Women faculty members may tend to favor women applicants or at least counter some of the negative attitudes displayed by faculties dominated by men. A school that hires women for its faculty is less negatively predisposed to admitting women students. Since a positive experience with women helps break down stereotypes, more women faculty are needed to improve the position of women graduate students. Also, schools with more women faculty probably are those with greater emphasis in the humanities and other "feminine" fields.

A negative sign in each equation on the variable indicates the proportion of the particular sex that is married and receiving a doctorate in a recent year. However, this coefficient is not statistically significant in the regression explaining acceptance rates for men. Why, then, is the negative relationship strong and significant between the proportion of recent married women doctoral recipients and the current acceptance rate for women? Perhaps those who make decisions on acceptances believe that married women doctorates are not committed to the labor force and, hence, represent "wasted" graduate school resources, since these students will not use their learning in a career.

Table 2.7 presents some simple correlations between job status upon receipt of the doctorate and percentage of married graduates of 222 doctorate-granting institutions. The first line shows the proportion of 1972 Ph.D. recipients who gave their postdoctoral status as "employed" at the time they received the doctorate. For men, the correlation is 0.3 between the percentage who are married and employed at graduation. (The units of observation are the institutions; numbers are for each institution as a whole.) Virtually no correlation (0.0036) appears between the percentage of women who are married and employed. Schools where a large portion of the men Ph.D. recipients are married are likely to have more men who have jobs when they receive their degrees. Schools where a relatively large proportion of the women degree recipients are married are neither more nor less likely than other schools to have more women graduates employed when they receive their degrees. Professors who help graduates find jobs may feel more compelled to assist married men. The feeling that it is more important for a married man than a married woman to work to support a family might indicate discrimination. However, it might also indicate that married women graduates feel less pressure to secure a job immediately upon graduation or that they find this a good time to "stop out" briefly and have their children.

These two explanations for the different rates of employment immediately upon receipt of the doctorate are standard: lack of help from professors, implying discrimination, and lack of motivation of women, implying that the differences are justified. However, the situation of most married women doctoral students might make contacts with professors difficult, for example, if more married women than single women or men attended school on a part-time basis. Even full-time married women students might have difficulty getting to know professors if they must get home immediately after class to meet children, or if their social lives are tied to their husbands' schedules

TABLE 2.7

Percentage of Married Ph.D. Recipients, by Job Status, 1972

Job Status	Mean Values		Simple Correlation with Proportion of Ph.D. Recipients Married	
	Men	Women	Men	Women
Employed	75.58	75.82	.3072	.0036
Signed contract, made definite commitment, negotiating	82.66	72.53	.4314	-.2177
Seeking appointment, no definite prospects	12.62	21.03	.0549	.2049
Other plans, no plans	.18	1.54	-.0504	.0294
Married	80.23	58.96		

and, hence, they are unable to attend extracurricular programs. In this situation, one should not blame professors for their inability to support married women in their job searches. On the other hand, if, as some have suggested, men faculty cultivate women colleagues in the hope of developing romantic interests, married women probably are perceived as having less potential in this regard. However, special efforts could be made to facilitate relationships as colleagues between married women students and their professors, perhaps by coffee hours at times convenient for women or office hours immediately before or after class.

Another barrier to married women may be that they move geographically to follow their husbands' careers. Educational continuity is interrupted, necessitating attendance at more than one graduate school before obtaining the doctorate. This, too, might reduce contacts with professors. However, the data reported in Chapter 4 indicate that men and women doctoral recipients (from 134 schools in 1972) are equally likely to have attended only one graduate institution (46 percent of each sex). Moreover, in explaining differences across institutions in the percentage of women graduates who attended only one graduate school, the percentage of married women graduates was a highly significant positive factor. Despite common perceptions, being married seems to be a positive influence on women.

The second line of Table 2.7 also reveals the percentage of graduates who, upon receipt of the degree, have either signed a contract, made a job commitment, or are negotiating with one or more potential employers. This group has a high probability of working soon after graduation. The simple correlation between percentage of degree recipients who are married men and this variable (for men) is 0.34, whereas the correlation between percentage of Ph.D. recipients who are married women and this variable (for women) is -0.22. Once again, lack of assistance or lack of urgency in securing a job might be a factor.

The third line distinguishes between the two reasons for differences in the first two lines. The correlation between the proportion of married men degree recipients and those who are seeking an appointment but have no definite prospects is 0.05, whereas the correlation for the corresponding group of women is 0.20. Apparently, married women are more likely than men to be seeking an appointment without any definite prospects. The sum of lines 2 and 3 for men does not differ much from the sum for women. That is, it appears that over 93 percent of both men and women who have recently received Ph.D. degrees would like to work, but a much larger proportion of the married women are not successful in job hunting.

The fourth line considers recent degree recipients who have plans other than full-time work. The correlation between the percentage of men recipients who are married and the percentage who do not intend to work is negative, whereas the correlation between the percentage of women degree recipients who are married and those who have plans other than employment is slightly positive.

In summary, schools with a larger proportion of married men graduates also have a larger proportion who are or will soon be employed. However, institutions with a relatively large proportion of married women graduates have a larger proportion who are having less success in their job searches. This lack of success is probably due less to the different motivations of men and women, since both either have been or are seeking employment in the same proportion, and due more to the greater futility of the women in securing jobs. The problem may encompass the oft-held view that married women (in contrast to single women or married men) do not need to work to support themselves or families.

Admissions committees may be more familiar with the fact that married women graduates are less likely to be working soon after they receive their degrees than with the reasons for this difference. The admissions committee may observe that women graduates are not working and infer a lack of desire or motivation on the part of women in general. Schools that award the same number of degrees to unmarried women probably do not have the same perception of a lower affinity for the labor market as schools with larger proportions of married women degree recipients. The admissions committee in a school where women are married, less supported in their job search, and less likely to be employed may infer that the reasons are inherent in the women, rather than in the placement officers. This being the case, admissions committees at institutions with greater proportions of married women receiving the doctorate might tend to discriminate against women, perceiving that they are less likely to be working upon completion of graduate school.

   The solution to this problem is twofold. First, those at the university should be made aware that women doctorates' lower employment rates are due less to motivation than to lack of assistance from professors. Rather than treating the problem by simply admitting fewer women, graduate schools might encourage faculty members to know their women students and provide equal assistance to men and women upon graduation. Whether or not employment after graduation is a valid consideration for admissions committees, apparently the differences in employment rates are used by admissions committees. In a sense, these decision makers are making the wrong decisions for the wrong reasons.

CONCLUSION

   The ratio of graduate school acceptances to applications is slightly greater for women than for men. A number of factors affect the admissions decision differently for women than for men, with certain variables given different weights by institutions when they consider applicants. Those making admissions decisions need more information so similar criteria will be used for both men and women. Apparently, there are no major differences in these decision-making processes that result in significantly fewer women being accepted. Whatever the problems in the admissions procedures, they are rather easily remedied.

3

**TIME SPENT IN
GRADUATE STUDY
BY MEN AND WOMEN
DOCTORAL RECIPIENTS**

One of the best sources of data on graduate students is the National Research Council's doctorate records files. Over 99 percent of all Ph.D.'s complete a questionnaire at the time they receive their degrees with information on time spent in graduate school NRC data on 1972 doctoral recipients are used here; these statistics apply only to those who have received the doctorate and not to those who have spent substantial time seeking this degree without success. A look at the average values of variables 1 to 5 in Table 3.1, by quality of institution, helps to explain the differences for men and women who attended different institutions.

A common belief is that women take longer than men to get their doctorates. The first variable, median age at Ph.D., lends some credence to this perception. However, at the best institutions, the median age at which men and women receive their degrees is virtually identical. The average age at Ph.D. rises as the quality of the institution awarding the degree declines. The range for men is from 29.02 years of age at the best institutions to 34 years at those of lowest quality. For women, the range is from 29.53 years for those at top institutions to 38.25 years for those at institutions with the lowest rating. The age gap between men and women who receive the doctorate widens dramatically from high- to low-quality institutions.

Age at Ph.D. is not a good indicator of the number of years an individual spends working toward his doctorate. Variables 2 and 3 clarify the age variable, providing a better idea of the time men and women invest for the Ph.D. Variable 2 presents statistics on the years elapsed between receipt of the bachelor's and the doctorate. Apparently, the years between the B.A. and the Ph.D. are greater for women than for men at every level of institutional quality. As in variable 1, the time lapse rises for both men and women as the quality of the institution awarding the degree declines. The lengthening of time is greater for

TABLE 3.1

The Calculation of Years in Graduate School

Institution (Roose-Andersen rating)	Median Age at Ph.D. (1)		Years Between B.A. and Ph.D. (2)		Median Years Not Enrolled from Graduate School Entrance to Ph.D. (3)		Years in Graduate School (2 - 3) (4)		Projected Entrance Lag (5)
	Men	Women	Men	Women	Men	Women	Men	Women	
4.0 - 3.496	29.02	29.53	6.71	7.56	0.52	0.78	6.20	6.78	.58
3.495 - 2.966	29.99	30.90	7.36	8.45	0.51	0.89	6.84	7.56	.72
2.995 - 2.496	30.47	32.38	7.58	9.20	0.60	1.21	6.97	7.99	1.02
2.495 - 1.996	31.35	33.83	8.26	10.11	0.78	1.49	7.49	8.61	1.12
1.995 - 1.496	31.80	34.97	8.73	10.55	0.94	1.72	7.79	8.83	1.04
1.495 - 0.996	32.79	38.37	9.38	12.84	1.51	2.85	7.87	9.99	2.10
Under 0.996	34.00	38.25	10.88	13.08	0.87	2.00	10.01	11.08	1.07
Not rated	32.16	37.23	8.92	12.15	1.46	2.94	7.46	9.33	1.89

women so that, at the best institutions, the time lapse for women exceeds that for men by less than one year, whereas at the lowest-rated institutions the difference is more than three years.

Centra (1974) has recently reached conclusions similar to those here. His data point out that time between receipt of bachelor's and doctoral degrees varies for members of both sexes according to field. Table 3.2 presents summary statistics from his survey. As Centra pointed out:

> The average ages, however, really don't tell the whole story. A higher percentage of women than men in all fields were under 25 when they received their doctorates, with the gap being especially notable in the humanities. Men were more likely to receive their degrees between the ages of 26 to 36, while more women received their doctorate after age 36. In fact, 43 percent of the women completed their degrees after age 37, compared to 28 percent of the men. Many of the older graduates, both men and women, were in education. The pattern for women in comparison to men, therefore, was to either go directly to graduate school after receiving their bachelor's degree, or more typically to obtain their doctorates later in life.
>
> The average number of years between receiving the bachelor's degree and the doctoral degree was about 13 for women and just under 11 for men. For every field, the average for women was greater than for men, varying from the physical sciences for which the average was about 8 for women and 7 for men, to education where the length of time between degrees was close to double this amount. For the biological sciences the averages were slightly greater than in the physical sciences: about 10 years between degrees for women and 8 for men. Women in both the humanities and social sciences averaged 13 years between degrees, men about 11 and 9 years respectively. Finally . . . there had not been a notable decrease in length of time between degrees: graduates in 1968 averaged about the same amount of time as those in 1950.
>
> In addition to the time spent working on a doctorate, the years between degrees could have been spent in several ways. For many women, it was a time for marriage and bearing and raising children; for men there were three wars—World War II, Korea, and Vietnam—that interrupted the progress of many. But undoubtedly most men and women spent the majority of their non-study time between degrees in professional employment. This is not to say, however, that these categories were mutually exclusive; many women, of course combined family with employment or doctoral

study, just as many men and women combined employment
and work toward a doctorate. In fact, about half of the
enrollments in graduate schools are part-time (pp. 22-25).

Since the interest is in actual time spent in pursuing the doctorate,
information is included on time not in attendance after beginning
graduate school. Variable 3 of Table 3.1 presents information on the
median number of years students graduating from each institution were
not enrolled between the time they entered graduate school and receipt
of the Ph.D. For a third time, the difference appears small at the best
institutions and increases as institutional quality declines, with the
increase in years not enrolled greater for women than for men. Hence,
the difference is virtually insignificant in the time not enrolled by men
and women at the best schools but more than a year at the lowest
rated institutions.

Variable 4 of Table 3.1 (variable 3 subtracted from variable 2)
approximates the actual time spent in graduate study. However, data
on the time between receipt of the B.A. and entrance into graduate
school were not available. Variable 4 would equal years of graduate
study if all those obtaining the Ph.D. entered graduate school immediately upon receipt of the bachelor's degree. Clearly this is not the
case, and variable 4 is biased upward because the time between receipt
of the bachelor's degree and graduate school entrance is not subtracted.
Even with this problem, the adjustment reduces the difference between
estimated time spent in graduate school by men and women. Looking at
graduates of successively lower-quality institutions, the time spent
still increases more slowly for men than for women, but the difference

TABLE 3.2

Average Number of Years Between Receipt of Bachelor's
and Doctoral Degrees

	Years	
	Women	Men
Humanities	12.9	11.3
Social Sciences	13.0	9.9
Biological Sciences	9.9	8.1
Physical Sciences	8.2	7.0
Education	16.6	13.8
All	13.1[a]	10.8[b]

Note: [a]N = 1,740. [b]N = 1,829
Source: J. A. Centra, Women, Men and the Doctorate (Princeton,
N.J.: Educational Testing Service, 1974), Table 3.2, p. 24.

between the estimated years of graduate school for men and women is smaller than either the age difference or the years elapsed between receipt of the B.A. and the doctorate. (It is more appropriate to deduct variable 3, years not enrolled, from variable 2, years between B.A. and Ph.D., than to deduct years of predoctoral employment, discussed below. Predoctoral work might have been combined with school and many women might have been out of school but not working for pay, staying home to raise children.)

Variable 5 is the difference between the values for men and women in variable 4. Assuming that men and women spend the same number of years in actual graduate study, Variable 5 would reflect the difference in delay by men and women in entering graduate school after receipt of the bachelor's. These differences do not appear unrealistic. Although no hard data are available to confirm the belief that women more often than men tend to delay entrance into graduate school, the perception exists. For example, Astin (1969) stated:

> A number of persons temporarily terminate their education at college graduation, work for a while (often because of financial need or because of a desire to take a break from the academic routine), and resume advanced training at a later date. . . . These patterns are particularly character-istic of women, who may interrupt their educations (as they do their careers) to marry and bear and raise children, and then reenter school at a later time, but frequently only on a part-time basis. Both these factors, then, help to account for the average twelve-year lapse between college graduation and doctorate completion that was found in the sample. . . . Only very few of the women in the sample (about 7 percent) started their graduate training immediately after baccalaureate completion and were able to complete the doctorate degree in four years (p. 20).

Cross (1972) found that of the "130,000 women who received the bachelor's degree in the spring of 1961, 72 percent expected to enter graduate school and three years later 42 percent had actually done some graduate work" (p. 31). It appears that many remaining women will enter graduate school at a still later date.

Of course, many men also do not enter graduate school immedi-ately upon receipt of the bachelor's degree. However, it is commonly held that a larger proportion of men do enter directly into graduate school. Hence, the average extra lag between B.A. completion and graduate school entrance of between one-half and two years seems realistic, and leads to the conclusion that in all likelihood women do not spend more time in actual graduate study than men despite the greater average age of women at the time they obtain the doctorate.

Apparently there is no direct way of estimating the time lag between graduation from college and entrance into graduate school. Most surveys enable calculation of the time lag between receipt of the B.A. and the Ph.D. but not of the lag in entering graduate school. However, it is possible to make several related calculations and draw some inferences by combining data from the National Center for Educational Statistics (NCES) with data on 1968 college freshmen from a survey conducted in August 1972 by the Cooperative Institutional Research Program (CIRP). The CIRP survey questionnaire asked respondents in late summer 1972 to indicate whether they were going to graduate school (presumably on either a part- or full-time basis) in fall 1972. Some 86,215 men and 44,288 women indicated that they intended to enter graduate school in fall 1972.

According to NCES statistics for fall 1972 on first-time enrollments in graduate school, 66,743 were first-time, full-time men students, while 44,437 were first-time, part-time men students, for a total enrollment of 111,180 men. Some 35,042 were first-time, full-time women students, while 36,758 were first-time, part-time women students, for a total enrollment of 71,800 women.

Combining CIRP and NCES figures, it appears that 86,215 of the 111,180 first-time men students were students who had begun college in 1968 and presumably completed it by June 1972. That is, 77.5 percent of first-time men students appear to have entered graduate school directly upon completion of bachelor's training. Similarly, 44,288 of the 71,800 first-time women students in graduate school appear to have been freshmen in 1968 who completed their bachelor's training by spring 1972. Some 61.7 percent of first-time women students apparently come directly from undergraduate training. Hence, 15.8 percent more first-time men students in graduate school come directly from undergraduate institutions. Over three-fourths of first-time men students come directly from undergraduate training, compared with only slightly more than 60 percent of women. This result is consistent with evidence that more women than men delay entrance to graduate school.

Table 3.3 explains differences by institution in these time-related variables by institutional characteristics. The regressions were run on data from 132 institutions for which all variables were available. Although all variables were included in the regressions, only significant coefficients are reported (F value greater than 2.0). Only those explanatory variables that exhibit a differential impact on men and women are discussed.

The first two regressions explain institutional differences in median age of doctoral recipients. As expected from Table 3.1, the institutional (Roose-Andersen) rating is a much greater factor in the age of women than of men. The increase in age at completion is much greater for women as quality of institution declines. Financial variables appear to affect women more than men. Even controlling for institutional

TABLE 3.3

Regressions to Explain Differences in Time Variables

Institutional Characteristics	Median Age at Ph.D.		Years Between B.A. and Ph.D.		Median Years not Enrolled, from Graduate School Entrance to Ph.D.		Difference Between Years Elapsed, B.A. to Ph.D., and Years not Enrolled	
	Men	Women	Men	Women	Men	Women	Men	Women
Roose-Andersen rating	- .679	- 1.481	- .496	- .824	- .322	- .386	-	- .4377
Total Ph.D.'s	.0089	.0111	.0069	.0095	.00168	.0017	.0052	.0078
Number of Ph.D.'s natural sciences	- .0147	- .021	- .0115	- .017	- .0026		- .0089	- .0139
Affluence code	- .24187	- .904	- .197	- .523	- .143	- .131		- .3924
Public/private	2.32547	2.727	1.112	2.344		.987	1.1398	1.356
GRE-verbal		- .023						- .0115
GRE-standard deviation	- .00008						- .00007	+ .00009
Percentage married	- .03371	- .0431			.0327			
Tuition			.00016					
Aid per student		- .901					- .3348	- .3866
Constant	31.459	48.486	10.029	17.004	- .23106	5.183	10.211	11.821
R²	.5099	.5721	.4772	.5070	.44405	.4134	.3803	.3916

Note: Regressions included the percentage of women faculty and the percentage of Ph.D.'s awarded to women; both were statistically insignificant.

quality, the coefficient on institutional affluence is almost four times
as large (negative direction) for women as for men; that is, although
both men and women receive their degrees at younger ages if they
attend wealthier institutions, this effect is much stronger for women.
Probably, at wealthier institutions women are provided with more support vis-a-vis men than at less wealthy institutions, which leads to a
more rapid completion of the degree. Even controlling for the general
affluence of the institution, the average aid per student has an additional negative effect, but only for women. That is, the larger the aid
per student, the younger the women doctoral recipients, the implication
being that women are more likely to persist in graduate school uninter-
rupted if they are provided with financial aid by the institution. One
reason might be their greater difficulty in getting external (noninstitutional) support.

Several other institutional variables affect the median age at
Ph.D. to roughly the same extent for men and women. Larger institutions, as reflected by the number of doctorates awarded, tend to have
older Ph.D. recipients. These institutions are probably less likely to
tailor programs to individual needs or to be concerned about practices
that reduce the time lag. Institutions focusing on the natural sciences
tend to have younger graduates. Neither the percentage of women on
the faculty nor the percentage of women doctoral recipients seems to
affect the median age of women.

Private graduate schools tend to award more doctorates to older
men and women than do public institutions. This finding is, of course,
derived from the regressions controlling for many other institutional
traits. Logically, the pattern could have been reversed, since high
tuition at private universities should provide an incentive to complete
studies as soon as possible. The simple correlation between the dummy
variable indicating whether an institution is public (variable = 1) or
private (variable = 2) is positive for men and negative for women.
Hence, although private institutions award degrees to younger women,
it is due to other variables in the regression, such as smaller size,
more money, and more aid. However, public institutions actually
award more degrees to younger men than do private institutions. Perhaps men who graduate from private institutions delay entrance to
graduate school to acquire the greater resources necessary.

The simple correlation between the public/private variable and
the time variables is:

		Control
Time lapse from B.A. to Ph.D.	M	.045
	F	-.006
Time between graduate school entrance and Ph.D.	M	-.099
	F	-.066

Both men and women are more likely to interrupt graduate training if they attend a private school, but men at private institutions have a longer overall lag between B.A. and Ph.D., which indicates a greater delay in starting graduate school.

If the average Graduate Record Examination (GRE) scores of applicants can be used as a measure of student quality, the better the student, the younger the age of graduation for women. After controlling for all other factors, this variables does not appear significant for men.

Institutions where a larger percentage of the men graduates were married have men whose median age is higher. However, institutions where a larger proportion of the women graduates were married are those where the median age is lower. This appears surprising, given the general belief that married women are less able to concentrate on their graduate work due to household and child responsibilities. However, institutions where a larger proportion of women were married also have women with fewer years of predoctoral work experience; that is, they were not working while in school. Married women doctoral recipients may work less during their graduate training, perhaps because they are supported by their spouses. Married men who receive the doctorate appear older, perhaps because they have had to work intermittently to support a family. Getting household help while a woman is in graduate school may be easier than finding alternate sources of family support in lieu of a married man student's job.

The second set of regressions in Table 3.3 explains years elapsed between receipt of the B.A. and the Ph.D. for men and for women. The results are similar to those from the first regression, with institutional quality having a greater effect in reducing the time lapse for women than for men, and affluence working in a similar way.

In the third set of regressions explaining median years not enrolled between graduate school entrance and receipt of the doctorate, the same variables appear to have roughly equal effects on men and women with one exception: the larger the proportion of men degree recipients who were married, the larger the time period not enrolled for men. This finding tends to confirm that married men at some time are forced to leave graduate school, probably to support a wife and child.

The fourth set of regressions has as its dependent variable the difference between years elapsed between receipt of the bachelor's and the doctorate and years not enrolled from graduate school entrance to receipt of the doctorate. The R^2 is lower in this set of regressions than in the first three sets, probably because the time lag between receipt of the doctorate and entrance into graduate school has been omitted. However, those graduating from better-quality institutions spend fewer years in graduate school; those attending larger institutions spend more time in graduate school; those at institutions with a higher proportion of doctorates in natural sciences spend less time in graduate

TABLE 3.4

Median Years of Predoctoral Experience

Institution (Roose-Andersen rating)	Men	Women
4.0 - 3.496	2.88	3.08
3.495 - 2.966	4.02	4.30
2.995 - 2.496	4.47	5.00
2.495 - 1.996	5.13	5.92
1.995 - 1.496	5.69	6.37
1.495 - 0.996	6.32	9.15
Under 0.996	7.64	7.54
Not rated	6.18	8.29

TABLE 3.5

Regressions to Explain Median Years of Predoctoral Experience

Institutional Characteristics	Men	Women
Roose-Andersen rating	- .596	- .898
Total Ph.D.'s	.00602	.007
Number of Ph.D.'s in natural sciences	- .00834	- .0123
Affluence code	- .22135	- .6167
GRE—verbal		- .031
GRE—standard deviation	- .00007	.00015
Percentage married		- .0374
Percentage of women faculty		
Percentage of women Ph.D.'s		
Tuition		
Aid per student	- .37737	- .525
Constant	10.3426	21.3414
R^2	.5794	.63777

school; and institutions awarding more aid per student have students who spend fewer years in graduate study.

Most significant, women do not appear to spend more time than men in graduate school to obtain the doctorate. The differences between time spent by men and women vary by institutional quality and other institutional characteristics. Apparently, women complete the doctorate much more rapidly at wealthier than at poorer institutions. They also complete the degree more rapidly if they are given more financial support. One way women are supported in graduate school is by their spouses' earnings. Despite earlier beliefs, married men appear more supportive of their wives in graduate school than married women are of their husbands. The different number of men and women who receive the doctorate is probably a major reason for the earlier misconception. Although many married men are supported by wives while in graduate school, this support is not systematically related to age at completion of the degree. The few married women who receive support from spouses seem to complete their doctorates early.

Table 3.4 provides data on median years of predoctoral experience for men and for women, while Table 3.5 explains differences for each sex among institutions by variables identical to those in Table 3.3. Women graduates at virtually every level of institutional quality have more years of predoctoral experience than men. This information came from a question about experience related to career and did not include time at home raising children. Women seem to interrupt their graduate training to work as well as to perform household activities. Most significant, women attending wealthier institutions and those that award more aid per student have fewer years of predoctoral experience. Although these variables have the same signs in the regression for men, the coefficients are much smaller. Women tend to work before receiving their doctorates to a greater extent than men, which may be explained partially by differences in financial aid awards. These findings are consistent with the discussion of the time variables above. Needed is more detail about why women appear to interrupt their graduate studies more frequently than men to work.

Arguments are sometimes made that women are treated as second-class citizens in graduate school, which causes them to take more time than men to complete their degrees. This treatment is exemplified by differential access to faculty time, fellowship aid, and study-related work. Difficulties imposed by rules on part-time status, credit transfers, and residency requirements are also alleged to impact with particular severity on women. Financial aid will be discussed in more detail below. However, the conclusion here is that, despite real or imaginary barriers, women do not spend significantly more time in school to obtain their doctorates. Of course, the suggested barriers may be hindering another group of women, namely, those who drop out before receipt of the doctorate.

4

**GEOGRAPHIC AND
INTERINSTITUTIONAL
MOBILITY OF MEN AND
WOMEN GRADUATE STUDENTS**

Two types of mobility—geographic and interinstitutional—figure in discussions of discrimination against women graduate students. The issue of geographic mobility is addressed here through data on NIH fellowship winners from the National Institutes of Health and on all graduate students from the National Center for Educational Statistics (NCES). Data on interinstitutional mobility from the National Research Council's doctorate records file are restricted to 1972 doctoral recipients.

Table 4.1 presents an analysis of students awarded predoctoral and postdoctoral fellowships by NIH in 1969. These students, after a rather rigorous screening by review committees, were deemed of the highest quality. Institutions are ranked in order of total number of NIH fellows attending. Data on the number of women at each institution are also presented. Although Columbia ranked tenth in attracting NIH fellows overall, it had the largest number of women NIH fellows. Harvard attracted the second largest number of women and the largest number of men. In general, highly qualified scholars seem to have access to the same types of institutions, regardless of sex. Those who survive the rigorous screening procedure of the fellowship competition will be accepted as scholars, rather than viewed as members of a particular sex.

The distribution of women appears more concentrated in universities in large urban centers. Of women recipients, ten percent selected institutions in New York City, whereas under four percent of men recipients chose institutions there. This distribution might indicate less sex discrimination in New York; however, women attend good graduate schools elsewhere. That women are forced to select institutions for graduate and postgraduate training in locations where their husbands also can attend college or obtain employment may explain this regional distribution. These women would be more likely to select large metropolitan centers and urban institutions over less populated locations, as they generally adjust to their husbands' careers.

TABLE 4.1

Leading 50 U.S. Institutions Chosen by National Institutes of Health Predoctoral and Postdoctoral Fellowship Awardees, 1969

First 25 Institutions	Total	Women	Second 25 Institutions	Total	Women
Harvard University	220	31	Case Western Reserve University	40	3
University of California, Berkeley	145	25	Princeton University	39	6
University of Wisconsin	142	13	California Institute of Technology	38	2
Stanford University	131	24	University of Texas	38	2
University of Washington	120	20	Pennsylvania State University	35	2
Cornell University	103	11	Boston University	33	12
Yale University	103	18	University of California, Davis	29	2
Massachusetts Institute of Technology	98	17	New York University	29	15
University of California, Los Angeles	85	16	University of North Carolina	28	10
Columbia University	76	33	Rockefeller University	28	3
University of Illinois	76	10	University of Pittsburgh	27	10
University of Michigan	72	4	Yeshiva University	27	4
Northwestern University	72	8	Washington University	26	4
University of California, San Diego	56	9	Brandeis University	24	4
University of Chicago	55	12	Iowa State University	24	2
University of Pennsylvania	53	7	University of Oregon	24	5
Duke University	52	7	State University of New York, Buffalo	24	1
Johns Hopkins University	52	7	University of California, Santa Barbara	23	5
University of Minnesota	50	6	University of Kansas	23	6
University of California, San Francisco	49	12	University of Utah	23	5
Indiana University	49	8	Baylor University	20	7
Michigan State University	49	5	University of Missouri	19	0
Purdue University	44	4	Oregon State University	19	1
University of Colorado	42	8	University of Alabama	18	1
Ohio State University	42	8	University of Iowa	18	1
First 25 Institutions	2,023	323 (15.9%)	Second 25 Institutions	676	113 (16.7%)
Percent of total U.S. fellows	56.3	57.2		18.8	20.0

Source: From Lewis C. Solmon, "Women In Doctoral Education: Clues and Puzzles Regarding Institutional Discrimination," Research In Higher Education 1 (1973): 319.

Some analysts have minimized this argument by pointing out that most women Ph.D.'s are unmarried. However, of all women who received a Ph.D. between 1958 and 1972, a total of 48.5 percent were married. During the same period, 78.4 percent of the men doctoral recipients were married (NRC). The proportion of married women is large enough to influence statistics on type of institution chosen by each sex if these choices were influenced by spouse's location.

The proportion of graduate students from each state who attend school outside their home state also provides evidence of mobility by sex. However, whether the greater movement by men to out-of-state schools is due to greater willingness to move or to constraints on women imposed from outside still cannot be determined. Since graduate students of both sexes have a propensity to attend a school outside their home state, the decision may be primarily in the hands of students rather than institutions. However, care must be taken in interpretation.

Table 4.2 reveals that more men than women from every single state leave their home states to attend graduate school. This finding cannot be attributed solely to discriminatory practices of high-quality institutions in other states against out-of-state women, since interstate moves to all institutions of all types are included.

Does this imply that men students are more efficient, better able to find the "best" institution for themselves without regard to geography? Possibly. Women might be more reluctant than men to leave home. Perhaps because the "investment" incurred locally in the search for a husband would be lost if they left the state for graduate school. If such is the case, they constrain the range of institutions from which they can choose and are probably most likely to make suboptimum choices.

To attend college away from home (out of state) is more expensive. Perhaps women (or their families) are less willing than men to incur the extra costs. If returns from education are higher for men regardless of where they attend college, then lower costs should be incurred for women's education to equalize rates of return. However, institutions may generally favor out-of-state men over out-of-state women in admissions. Moreover, since out-of-state attendance is more costly, students going out of state might have to borrow to finance the move. It is probably easier for men to borrow and hence to move. Moreover, fewer women may get financial aid.

It is frequently argued that one problem women face as graduate students is overmobility: They must switch colleges to follow their husbands, who move throughout their careers. Table 4.3 gives the proportion of 1972 men and women doctoral recipients who have attended only one graduate school. These are the people who are ultimately successful in graduate school, that is, those who receive the doctorate. From among this select group, however, it appears that women are more likely than men who graduate from comparable institutions to attend only one graduate school. In most cases, differences are not statistically significant. Possibly the belief about overmobility

TABLE 4.2

Graduate Students by Sex and by Home State, All Institutions, 1968

State	Men				Women			
	Total Number in State	Total Number from State in State	Number Out of State	Percentage Out of State	Total Number in State	Total Number from State in State	Number Out of State	Percentage Out of State
Alabama	3,952	2,632	1,320	33.40	2,258	1,715	543	24.04
Alaska	276	91	185	67.02	155	96	59	38.06
Arizona	5,276	4,458	818	15.50	3,223	3,051	272	8.18
Arkansas	1,818	778	1,040	57.20	1,072	738	334	31.15
California	58,204	51,049	7,155	12.29	33,340	31,207	2,133	6.39
Colorado	5,993	4,480	1,513	25.24	3,391	2,937	454	13.38
Connecticut	10,704	7,248	3,456	32.28	3,307	6,987	1,320	15.89
Delaware	1,448	734	714	49.30	631	421	210	33.28
District of Columbia	2,991	2,080	911	30.45	2,044	1,553	491	24.02
Florida	10,794	8,068	2,726	25.25	6,121	5,086	1,035	16.90
Georgia	5,075	3,564	1,511	29.77	2,889	2,277	612	21.18
Hawaii	2,254	1,675	579	25.68	3,000	2,670	723	24.10
Idaho	1,391	460	931	66.93	557	321	236	42.36
Illinois	27,628	20,542	7,086	25.64	14,462	12,010	2,452	16.95
Indiana	11,874	9,416	2,458	20.70	8,318	7,493	825	9.91
Iowa	5,821	3,606	2,215	38.05	2,748	1,838	910	33.11
Kansas	5,300	3,317	1,983	37.41	3,009	2,186	823	27.35
Kentucky	4,312	2,680	1,632	37.84	3,062	2,302	760	24.82
Louisiana	5,696	4,227	1,469	25.79	4,271	3,706	565	13.22
Maine	1,256	643	613	48.80	610	362	248	40.65
Maryland	11,420	5,382	6,038	52.87	6,339	4,351	1,988	31.36
Massachusetts	18,156	13,860	4,296	23.66	8,850	7,249	1,601	18.09

State							
Michigan	20,567	17,601	2,966	14.42	12,284	11,256	1,028	8.36
Minnesota	7,452	4,916	2,536	34.03	2,722	1,856	866	31.81
Mississippi	2,473	1,612	861	34.81	1,656	1,289	367	22.16
Missouri	9,220	6,620	2,600	28.19	5,276	4,134	1,142	21.64
Montana	1,481	826	655	44.22	417	237	180	43.16
Nebraska	3,302	2,204	1,098	33.25	1,796	1,446	350	19.48
Nevada	852	530	322	37.79	506	422	84	16.60
New Hampshire	1,251	327	924	73.86	468	159	309	66.02
New Jersey	23,615	12,699	10,916	46.22	10,786	7,089	3,697	34.27
New Mexico	2,765	1,999	766	27.70	1,352	1,121	231	17.08
New York	75,239	61,410	13,829	18.38	47,894	42,909	4,985	10.40
North Carolina	5,266	3,589	1,677	31.84	3,343	2,690	653	19.53
North Dakota	1,112	562	550	49.46	443	243	200	45.14
Ohio	20,610	15,282	5,328	25.85	9,446	7,525	1,921	20.33
Oklahoma	5,345	4,115	1,230	23.01	3,462	3,041	421	12.16
Oregon	7,006	5,574	1,432	20.43	4,641	4,150	491	10.57
Pennsylvania	30,889	22,878	8,011	25.93	15,968	13,094	2,874	17.99
Rhode Island	2,862	1,938	924	32.28	1,986	1,613	373	18.78
South Carolina	2,303	1,272	1,031	44.76	1,310	880	430	32.82
South Dakota	1,289	652	637	49.41	532	303	229	43.04
Tennessee	5,923	4,419	1,504	25.39	3,268	2,692	576	17.62
Texas	20,233	16,771	3,462	17.11	11,347	10,203	1,144	10.08
Utah	3,872	2,998	874	22.57	1,219	1,066	153	12.55
Vermont	777	303	474	61.00	337	145	192	56.97
Virginia	9,752	4,374	5,378	55.14	4,663	2,755	1,908	40.91
Washington	6,188	4,181	2,007	32.43	2,943	2,289	654	22.22
West Virginia	1,938	1,135	803	41.43	1,305	967	338	25.90
Wisconsin	9,544	6,892	2,647	27.73	4,682	3,858	824	17.59
Wyoming	616	263	353	57.30	252	139	113	44.84

Source: G. H. Wade, Residence and Migration of College Students (Washington, D.C.: National Center for Educational Statistics, 1968).

79

TABLE 4.3

Percentage of Doctoral Recipients Attending
One Graduate School, 1972

Institution (Roose-Andersen rating)	Men	Women
4.0 - 3.496	64.32	64.06
3.495 - 2.996	53.81	50.81
2.995 - 2.496	48.31	50.30
2.495 - 1.996	46.63	46.17
1.995 - 1.496	44.66	48.43
1.495 - 0.996	40.64	41.05
Under 0.996	38.50	44.45
Not rated	45.12	49.91

TABLE 4.4

Regressions Explaining Percentage Attending
Only One Graduate School

Institutional Characteristics	Percentage Attending One Graduate School	
	Men	Women
Roose-Andersen rating	2.1554	4.507
Total Ph.D.'s	- .017	- .022
Number of Ph.D.'s in natural sciences	.044	.0474
Affluence code	—	—
Public/private	—	-10.464
GRE—verbal	—	—
GRE—standard deviation	—	- .0004
Percentage married	- .176	.145
Percentage women faculty	—	—
Percentage women Ph.D.'s	-16.895	20.696
Tuition	—	.0065
Aid per student	2.271	3.354
Constant	66.402	80.869
R^2	.4986	.3729

originates because women who do not successfully complete their graduate training with a doctorate fail primarily because they have moved, that is, switched colleges to follow their husbands. Unfortunately, here, as in several other cases, no data on noncompleters are available. The proportion attending only one graduate school declines with the quality of institution attended. A student probably switches more frequently to a lower quality than to a higher quality institution.

Table 4.4 assesses institutional differences in number of graduates attending only one institution by the variables used in regressions in Chapter 3. The much stronger relationship between quality of degree-granting institution and proportion of women who attended only one graduate school, compared with the relationship for men, implies substantially less movement by women than by men among institutions with different characteristics. Larger institutions that award more Ph.D.'s have relatively smaller proportions of one-institution doctoral recipients. Similarly, those that grant a large proportion of their Ph.D.'s in the natural sciences have a larger proportion of graduates who attend only one institution. Institutions awarding more aid per student also have more graduates who attend a single graduate school.

Two independent variables demonstrate sign reversals between the regressions for men and women. Apparently, the higher the proportion of men doctoral recipients who are married, the lower the proportion of graduates who attend only one institution: that is, for men, interinstitutional movement seems significantly related to being married. However, the reverse appears true for women: Institutions with a larger proportion of married women graduates have a larger proportion of graduates who attend only that one institution. Once again, in opposition to the "camp follower" theory of married women students, marriage is more a stabilizer for women than for men. Institutions awarding a larger proportion of doctorates to women have a larger proportion of recipients who attend a single graduate institution. Apparently, women who attend institutions that give numerous degrees to women tend to remain there. However, men who attend those institutions are more likely to have attended more than one institution, a finding reflected by the negative coefficient on the variable for percentage of doctorates awarded to women in the regression for men.

Three additional variables are significant in the regression for women but not in that for men. The negative sign on the coefficient of the dummy variable indicating public or private institution implies that graduates of public institutions are less likely to have attended only one graduate school; that is, women are more likely to transfer from a private to a public institution than to move the other way. In the regression dealing with women doctoral recipients, the coefficient on the tuition variable is positive, indicating that the institutions with high tuition are more likely to have a large number of graduates who attended a single institution. On the premise that a good deal of moving is due to financial problems, one would not expect moves from low- to high-tuition institutions, but rather the opposite, which the regression indicates.

Conclusions about the relative mobility of men and women graduate students are mixed. Looking at groups of graduate students who have not yet received the doctorate, it appears that (1) the best women students select institutions in fewer geographic locations than men do and (2) more men than women attend graduate school out of state.

If the reasons postulated for these differences pertain to predoctoral students, they appear irrelevant in explaining interinstitutional mobility of successful doctoral students. On the one hand, being married appears to stabilize women, rather than having the reverse effect. On the other hand, financial problems appear to restrict geographic mobility but to increase interinstitutional mobility of women students.

5

AWARDING FINANCIAL AID TO MEN AND WOMEN GRADUATE STUDENTS

Thus far, this study has found no significant differences by sex in admissions policies of graduate schools. Neither do women spend more time than men in graduate school, nor are they substantially hindered by problems of mobility. A major perception remaining is that women are discriminated against in financial aid. This view, like others, has generally been supported by anecdotal evidence, while definitions of the issue have varied.

To explicate the issues relevant to determining if discrimination by sex is involved in awarding financial aid, several questions must be answered:

1. How many men and women graduate students receive aid, measured in terms of numbers of awards; the proportion to those of each sex enrolled who get awards; and the proportion to those of each sex who apply who get awards?

2. What is the amount of aid per award to members of each sex?

3. Does the type of aid—nonservice awards versus awards with work requirements, research versus teaching assistantships, grants versus loans—differ by sex?

4. Are aggregate differences the result of sex or of different amounts of funds available by field?

Financial aid, an important determinant of an individual's success during his graduate years, has obvious value in providing support and sustenance. A student with aid is generally not required (or at times even allowed) to find other means to support himself or his family that would detract from his studies. Clearly, large nonservice awards enable the graduate student to devote more time to his studies. Even awards that require work are probably relevant to a student's study plan or ultimate career objectives. These would tend to complement rather than detract from his pursuit of the doctorate. Also, a student with greater resources may be able to purchase nonrequired reference books or better housing with comfortable study facilities, both helpful in pursuing a doctorate.

In addition to the sheer value of financial aid dollars, awards generally serve a second purpose: They give recipients a clear indication that groups within the university (professors and administrators) deem them a worthy investment; that is, think they are of superior merit and will be successful in their pursuit of the doctorate. Most prople with graduate school experience can probably recall that a status division occurs between those on fellowships and those financing their own education. If indeed one of the barriers to equal success in graduate school for women is a lack of confidence and encouragement, one measurement of lower-level encouragement is the pattern of financial aid awards. A most effective way to indicate to a woman graduate student that the faculty views her as a competent student equal to the men in the class is to award her financial aid. The first value of financial aid—what the money can buy—will have an impact directly proportional to the size of the award. The second value—encouragement and confidence—might be fostered merely by making the award, regardless of its dollar value. Those making awards probably place a disproportionate emphasis on need to the exclusion of the psychological contribution. Once this second value is recognized, some modification in awards could lead to more efficient use of a given dollar amount.

A third way that financial aid may impact is by bringing students into contact with faculty. Students awarded either teaching or research assistantships are brought face to face with particular faculty members to perform their jobs. The value of getting to know faculty is great: contacts might lead to faculty becoming role models, providing encouragement during the trials and tribulations of graduate study, suggesting courses and areas of research, and finally, providing assistance to students seeking postdoctoral employment. None of these services is available to a student who does not know any faculty members. Although many of these functions can be performed by a faculty member supervising either a teaching or a research assistant, some evidence (Astin 1975) indicates that research assistantships are more effective for students than teaching assistantships. Teaching assistants generally teach low-level undergraduate courses that do not complement their graduate studies. However, research assistants are generally involved in research projects with a professor who can teach about research methods in a practical way, suggest additional topics for the student to pursue, perhaps for his doctoral thesis, and include topics that supplement work done for courses.

Table 5.1 presents some experiences of men and women graduate students concerning financial aid. Experiences are from a 1971 followup survey of 1961 college freshmen who subsequently attended graduate school (El-Khawa and Bisconti 1974). In response to questions about

TABLE 5.1

Financial Experiences of Graduate Students, by Sex, 1971
(percentages); responses from 1961 freshmen

Experience	Total	Men	Women
Financial situation			
Had a major concern for meeting expenses	29	31	25
Received much less financial assistance			
than I needed	11	12	9
A fellowship was not renewed when expected	1	2	1
Worked (or expect to work) on thesis off			
campus while employed full time	16	16	17
Worked (or expect to work) on thesis as part			
of my employment on a research project	8	9	5
Obstacles to completing study			
Loss of fellowship, scholarship, traineeship	1	1	1
Other financial problems	15	15	14
Family obligations	18	15	24
Duties involved in a teaching assistantship	3	3	2
Duties involves in a research assistantship	1	1	1
Administration of a stipend	1	*	1
Reasons for interrupting study			
Took a job	42	44	38
Home/child care responsibilities	28	17	44
No fellowship (scholarship, grant) offered	5	4	6
Fellowship, etc., terminated	2	2	1
Other financial problems	16	16	17

*Less than 0.5.
Source: Elaine H. El-Khawas and Ann S. Bisconti, Five and Ten
Years After College Entry (Washington, D.C.: American Council on
Education, 1974), pp. 123-26.

their financial situation in graduate or professional school, 31 percent
of the men but only 25 percent of the women had a major concern for
meeting expenses. Similarly, 12 percent of the men and 9 percent of
the women received much less financial assistance than they needed.
There was virtually no difference in the proportion of men and women
for whom a fellowship was not renewed when expected (2 percent of
men and 1 percent of women) or who worked or expected to work on the

thesis off-campus while employed full time (16 percent of the men and
17 percent of the women). However, 9 percent of the men but only 5
percent of the women worked or expected to work on a thesis as part of
their employment on a research project. Statistically significant differences between men and women in their overall concern with financial
aid are virtually nonexistent. However, financial aid comes to men
somewhat more often than to women through employment in research.

Differences also were virtually nonexistent in the number of men
and women who reported as obstacles loss of fellowship, scholarship,
or traineeship, other financial problems, duties involved in a teaching
or research assistantship, or administration of stipend. However, 15
percent of the men but 24 percent of the women thought family obligations a serious obstacle to completing graduate study. Although family obligations are an important obstacle for both men and women, more women
are burdened with family responsibilities. This finding is consistent
with earlier speculation that men might be more concerned with raising
money to maintain a family, whereas women are more concerned with
running the family itself. To men, financial problems and family obligations were equally important obstacles, whereas women found family
obligations an obstacle 10 percentage points more often. It is difficult
to blame the universities for this situation, although creating day-care
centers and the like would solve part of the women's problem. However,
this begs the question of why women rather than men are left with the
family responsibilities, a condition probably due more to social mores
than to anything the university does or does not do.

Some 44 percent of the men interrupted graduate study to take a
job, whereas 44 percent of the women interrupted their studies for home
and child-care responsibilities. Some 38 percent of the women ceased
their studies to take a job, while only 17 percent of the men stopped
because of home and child-care responsibilities. These findings give
further weight to the discussion above. Slightly more women than men
interrupted their studies because they were not offered a fellowship.
However, the proportion of both men and women who gave this reason
was small. Even fewer men and women stopped their studies because
their fellowships terminated. Finally, an equal number of men and
women interrupted their studies because of other financial problems.

Table 5.2 presents information from 1966 college freshmen who
enrolled for advanced study about why they did not enroll in their first-
choice graduate or professional school. Some 61 percent of the men
but only 30 percent of the women did not enroll at their first-choice
institution because they were not accepted, a finding that confirms the
conclusions about admissions practices. However, 25 percent of the
women but only 11 percent of the men did not enroll because they
received no offers of financial assistance. Perhaps one reason why
women did not seem worse off than men in terms of financial aid is
that women attend lower-quality institutions, which are more likely to
offer them aid. Men will in all likelihood be offered aid at better

TABLE 5.2

Reasons of 1966 Freshmen for Not Enrolling at First-Choice Graduate or Professional School, by Sex and Field (percentages)

Reasons	Total	Men	Women	Graduate Field				
				Biological Sciences	Physical Sciences and Mathematics	Health Fields	Social Sciences	Other Fields
Was not accepted	50	61	30	55	43	74	57	51
No financial aid offered	16	11	25	23	30	4	18	17
Unacceptable amount of financial assistance offered	5	4	5	4	13	4	1	4
Better terms of financial assistance at second-choice school	9	7	12	1	17	2	12	10
Other reasons (not financial)	31	24	44	25	23	23	26	34
Total number not enrolled at first-choice institution	53,337	35,320	18,017	2,243	3,590	5,324	6,873	31,126
Percentage of total	19	21	15	24	23	21	35	16

Source: Elaine H. El-Khawa and Ann S. Bisconti, Five and Ten Years After College Entry (Washington, D.C.: American Council on Education, 1974), p. 134.

TABLE 5.3

Number of Women Fellowship Applicants and Recipients, by Field, 1963-68

Field	Applicants			Recipients		
	Total	Number of Women	Percentage of Women	Total	Number of Women	Percentage of Women
Physical sciences	7,717	359	4.65	2,140	163	7.61
Social sciences[a]	9,801	955	9.74	2,187	388	17.74
Arts and humanities	8,403	1,180	14.04	1,927	294	15.25
Professional[b]	548	49	8.94	4,618	337	7.29
Education[c]	23,659	8,160	34.49	6,299	2,637	41.86
Unclassified[d]	66,778	12,722	19.05	105,356	22,857	21.69

a3,835 applications, 485 recipients not categorized by sex.
b2,854 applications not categorized by sex.
c950 applicants not categorized by sex.
d49,542 applicants not categorized by sex.

Source: C. L. Atwood, Women in Fellowship and Training Programs (Washington, D.C.: Association of American Colleges, 1972).

institutions. Table 5.2 supports this view: Institutions other than
their first choice offered aid to women on better terms. Only 15 percent of the women but 21 percent of the men did not enroll at their
first-choice institutions. Again this confirms that women probably aim
lower than men for reasons involving financial aid distribution.

Although Table 5.1 supports the conclusion that women graduate
students are not much more burdened by financial aid problems than
men, one cannot conclude that no differential treatment exists. Women
apparently aim for less prestigious or at least different institutions,
presumably those less preferred, to guarantee that financial aid problems will not hinder them. Eliminating discrimination might produce
the same responses found in Table 5.1 but it would enable women to
apply and enroll at institutions of higher quality.

The proportion of women students applying for fellowship aid
differs from the proportion actually receiving it. Table 4.7 compares
fellowship applications and awards of women with those of all applicants. These data summarize a report by Attwood (1972) on all fellowship programs for which statistics existed during the academic years
1968-69 to 1972-73. In virtually all except the professional fields,
women comprise a larger share of recipients than of applicants. In
some cases, awards are made to women in about the same proportion
as they apply. Although, at first glance, this finding might refute
arguments over discrimination in awarding fellowships, perhaps only a
few top-quality women apply. Almost all men students apply for awards.

Table 5.4 presents the proportion of full-time graduate women
students in doctoral science departments, including social sciences,
and the proportion of women, compared with men, financing studies by
various means. For example, 1.3 percent of the aeronautical engineering enrollment is women and precisely 1.3 percent of the institutional
support goes to women. Similarly, 1.2 percent of those in aeronautical
engineering who rely on themselves, loans, and families for support
are women. The "institutional support" and "self, loans, and family"
columns, of primary importance here, give the proportion of institutional funds awarded to women and the proportion of women who sustain
themselves by borrowing or by personal resources.

In most engineering specializations, the proportion of institutional support awarded to women is greater than the proportion of women
in the specialization. In several fields where this is not the case,
women receive a disproportionately large share of U.S. government
awards. Moreover, in the engineering fields, a smaller proportion of
women support themselves by loans or family resources than the proportion of women in the field. This is also true of the physical sciences
and mathematics. However, in life sciences, where they represent a
much larger proportion of students, women receive a smaller share of
institutional and government support than one would predict, assuming
that share is equal to the proportion of women students. Similarly, a
larger proportion of women rely on loans and family support, a pattern

TABLE 5.4

Proportion of Financial Aid Awards to Women, by Field and Type

Field	Percentage of Women in Field	HEW	Other U.S. Government	Institutional Support	Self, Loans, and Family	Other U.S. Sources	Foreign Sources	All Sources
Engineering								
Aeronautical	1.3	0	.012	.013	.012	.017	0	.012
Agricultural	.2	0	0	.018	.030	.071	0	.017
Chemical	2.5	.042	.026	.028	.041	.016	.043	.029
Civil	3.0	.043	.027	.023	.020	.024	.036	.025
Electrical	2.2	.037	.014	.022	.019	.015	.015	.019
Engineering science	2.9	.029	.026	.030	.057	.031	0	.031
Industrial	5.6	.058	.014	.094	.028	.104	.035	.044
Mechanical	1.3	.010	.012	.010	.011	.005	.023	.011
Metallurgical	3.5	.066	.035	.031	.005	.016	.028	.028
Mining	2.8	0	.034	.019	.026	0	.100	.027
Nuclear	1.4	0	.018	.027	.014	0	.029	.018
Petroleum	2.2	0	.069	0	0	0	0	.009
Other	5.8	.052	.036	.044	.077	.038	.037	.052
Physical sciences								
Astronomy	10.1	.188	.076	.108	.145	.071	0	.100
Atmospheric	5.7	0	.048	.065	.056	.111	.190	.057
Chemistry	15.2	.161	.112	.161	.180	.151	.114	.153
Geosciences	10.9	.105	.087	.113	.112	.092	.008	.102
Oceanography	10.9	.154	.090	.134	.109	.127	.182	.108
Physics	6.3	.091	.041	.072	.079	.044	.064	.061

Mathematics								
Applied	14.0	.095	.086	.150	.158	.161	.091	.137
Mathematics	19.0	.188	.116	.200	.219	.244	.101	.196
Statistics	19.7	.246	.188	.189	.266	.117	.219	.211
Life sciences								
Agricultural	8.6	.300	.106	.117	.159	.128	.055	.134
Biochemistry	24.7	.186	.171	.225	.300	.259	.235	.208
Biology	32.3	.315	.247	.289	.322	.289	.270	.299
Botany	24.6	.231	.185	.230	.257	.149	.113	.220
Microbiology	32.4	.299	.268	.261	.385	.275	.174	.293
Pharmacology	19.4	.156	.113	.134	.321	.019	.261	.164
Physiology	20.7	.219	.256	.249	.225	.182	.154	.230
Zoology	22.7	.306	.153	.231	.207	.128	.267	.219
Other	29.6	.301	.167	.212	.266	.146	.090	.238
Psychology	36.3	.372	.275	.341	.400	.318	.353	.357
Social sciences								
Agricultural economics	7.1	0	.040	.066	.097	.012	.102	.060
Anthropology	44.2	.422	.333	.383	.445	.393	.409	.413
Economics	12.4	.164	.087	.115	.136	.103	.084	.119
Geography	21.6	.133	.127	.174	.165	.127	.167	.163
History and philosophy of science	25.0	.256	.167	.231	.282	.137	.125	.243
Linguistics	48.0	.502	.386	.449	.509	.477	.410	.468
Political science	18.0	.246	.189	.184	.168	.209	.105	.181
Sociology	18.2	.367	.278	.363	.370	.341	.218	.355
Sociology and anthropology	36.5	.449	.289	.415	.464	.250	.167	.425

Source: Survey on graduate science student support, conducted by the National Science Foundation, 1972.

91

that persists in the social sciences, where women receive smaller shares of institutional and government awards relative to their share of the student body and rely more than men on loans and family support.

In terms of numbers of awards to men and women, Table 5.4 shows that women do well in fields where they are relatively under-represented in the study body, such as engineering, physical sciences, and mathematics. However, in fields where they have a higher representation, such as life sciences and social sciences, women receive a smaller share of government and institutional funds than their share of the student body.

In the so-called "masculine" fields, perhaps only exceptionally able women enroll in doctoral programs. These capable women are visible and, hence, get the awards they deserve. The criteria for predicting success in these fields are also more objective (such as mathematical aptitude tests). Again, women in these fields may apply to institutions that are not of the highest quality and, hence, compete with less able men. However, in life and social sciences the quality and aptitude of the women vary and a larger proportion of the less-than-top-notch are bypassed for awards. Also, women may apply to more competitive graduate schools and be rejected for awards when they are compared with equally qualified or more capable men. In any case, it is in precisely those fields where women are underrepresented that they receive the most in financial aid awards.

Outside the physical sciences, where the proportion of awards is the same for men and women (Table 5.1) but the awards per student are smaller for women (Table 5.4), the fellowship application rate for women is lower:

$$\frac{\text{Awards}}{\text{Applicants}} \cdot \frac{\text{applicants}}{\text{enrollees}} = \frac{\text{awards}}{\text{enrollees}}$$

Hence:

$$\frac{\text{applicants}}{\text{enrollees}} = \frac{\text{awards}}{\text{enrollees}} \bigg/ \frac{\text{awards}}{\text{applicants}}$$

Since, in the second equation, the numerator is lower and the denominator is higher for women in the social and life sciences, the application rate for aid by women is lower. In the physical sciences and engineering, where both the awards/applicants rate and the awards/enrollees rate are higher for women, one cannot say that fewer enrolled women apply for aid. Probably, the few women enrolled in these fields all apply or apply in the same proportion as men. Some women in these fields may think they are not qualified for or would not get aid, even though this view may be a misconception.

Table 5.5 aggregates for all fields some of the data presented in Table 5.4. Keep in mind that 18.9 percent of the total graduate

TABLE 5.5

Support Sources for Graduate Science Students, by Sex, Fall 1972

Source of Support	Men	Women	Percentage of Women
Total U.S. government (excluding loans)	37,733	7,296	16.20
Institutional	47,510	10,374	17.92
Other U.S. sources	7,940	1,409	15.07
Foreign sources	2,805	273	8.87
Total nongovernment (excluding personal sources)	58,255	12,056	17.10
Self, loans, and family	27,357	7,240	20.93
Total	123,345	26,592	17.74

Source: Survey on graduate science student support, conducted by the National Science Foundation, 1972.

students in this study were women. Some 16.2 percent of the total U.S. government awards, excluding loans, are made to women, a percentage less than their representation in the student body. Similarly, 17.9 percent of the institutional support, 15.1 percent of other U.S. sources, 8.9 percent of foreign sources, and 17.1 percent of the total nongovernment sources, excluding personal resources, are awarded to women. In all cases, a smaller proportion of awards are made to women than one would predict from their 18.9 percent share of the student body, assuming that men and women receive awards in proportion to enrollment. (Remember, most women are in life or social sciences.) Similarly, almost 21 percent of those supporting themselves by loans or personal sources are women, a percentage slightly higher than their representation in the student body. Only 17.74 percent of the total support goes to women, implying that roughly 1 percent of the women did not report the type of aid they received. Although women do somewhat less well than one would predict by enrollment, the overall figures are not much different for men and women. These results differ significantly by field.

So far, the focus has been on numbers of awards rather than on dollar value or type. Until this time, virtually no data sources have been available for average dollar values or types of awards by sex. In the survey of graduate deans (see Chapter 2), a section on financial aid was included. Far fewer deans were able to provide information on financial aid than on acceptance rates. Table 4.10 summarizes data for the institutions reporting on financial aid—about 50 in all. Although the number of responses is small and perhaps nonrepresentative, these

TABLE 5.6

Distribution of Financial Aid by Type and Amount, 1972

	Proportion of Enrollment Receiving Awards		Average Dollar Value of Award			
			Direct Stipend		Tuition and Fee Waiver	
	Men	Women	Men	Women	Men	Women
Total nonservice awards	.115	.138	2389	2270	1579	1446
Awarded by Institution						
Fellowships or scholarships	.081	.087	2309	2280	1353	1392
Traineeships	.028	.043	2608	2472	2114	1761
Other	.048	.042	2955	2799	1244	1179
Awarded by external (other) sources	.043	.040	2587	2442	1545	1519
Total service awards (other nonrepayable aid)	.306	.245	2648	2536	1311	1302
Research assistantships	.120	.079	2647	2638	1274	1337
Teaching assistantships	.219	.224	2501	2476	1260	1255
Other graduate assistantships	.072	.079	2561	2472	1128	1132
Instructorships	.069	.092	5037	3388	705	1000
Other	.101	.043	2362	2276	1206	1214
Institutional loans	.119	.136				
GI bill	.193	.027				

Source: Survey of graduate deans in which 50 schools provided usable statistics.

are the only available data on the subject; the patterns are consistent, tending to confirm some of the hypotheses.

Table 4.10 gives the proportion of those enrolled who receive various awards. Enrollments are for the institutions that provided financial aid statistics in the deans' survey. Some 13.8 percent of the women and 11.5 percent of the men received nonservice awards. A few more women received fellowships or scholarships and traineeships. A significantly larger share of men received other nonservice awards and awards from noninstitutional (external) sources.

Some 30.6 percent of the men and 24.5 percent of the women received awards for service. A significantly larger share of the men received research assistantships, a condition that might be a barrier for women, since work on a research project is a most valuable graduate experience. A slightly larger proportion of women received service awards, which included teaching (teaching assistantships, other graduate assistantships, and instructorships). The catchall residual category "other service awards" had 10 percent of the men but only slightly more than 4 percent of the women.

Slightly more women than men receive loans and, as expected, a far larger share of men attend graduate school with GI benefits.

A look at the proportion receiving awards does not indicate that women are at a disadvantage, except when they are excluded from research assistantships. The differential availability of research assistantships by field and their absence in fields in which women usually enroll may be a factor here.

In terms of the average dollar value of the stipend, the difference between awards to men and women is surprisingly small. In virtually every case, men receive a slightly larger stipend than women, but the difference is rarely more than several hundred dollars. The exception is instructorships, where payment to men is generally several thousand dollars more. One might question the difference in definition between instructorship and teaching assistantship. A teaching assistantship probably involves teaching class sections of courses led by senior professors, whereas an instructorship probably involves teaching independently at an intermediate undergraduate level. If this is the case, men are probably given fuller responsibilities in teaching intermediate-level courses or allowed to teach more often; thus, instructorships for men result in larger payments.

The average value of tuition and fee waivers is also similar for men and women. In most cases, the value of these waivers is almost identical for both—all fees waived or no fees waived. The observation that men receive higher tuition and fee waivers probably arises because men attend more expensive institutions. This argument also supports speculation that men apply to the highest-quality (perhaps private) institutions.

It is generally argued that the same proportion of women receive awards but that many times women are deemed less needy than men who have a responsibility to support a family. Therefore, women are given smaller awards. This argument receives no support from the sample here. Although it could be that only those institutions that do not discriminate are willing to provide data, from these data there is no way to determine the reasons for the similar stipends. The American Psychological Association (1972) also found stipends approximately equal for men and women students in psychology. Of course, differences of several hundred dollars could give evidence of discrimination rather than of equal treatment. Chapter 4 indicated that women are more likely than men to attend graduate schools in urban areas where living costs are higher. However, that women tend to receive lower tuition and fee waivers as well implies that overall they attend less costly institutions where stipends and tuition are lower. The argument of differential value of fellowships has generally been based on allegations of differences in value of awards, such that men receive two or three times as much as women, rather than several hundred dollars difference on a base of several thousand dollars.

A slightly larger proportion of women obtained institutional loans. It has been argued that women might be less inclined to take out large loans. First, since women experience lower earnings in the labor force, it is more difficult for them to repay a loan. Second, a loan, in a sense, represents a negative dowry; some think a woman might have more difficulty getting married if her "trousseau" included significant debt obligations. Remember, more men than women are already married during graduate training. Table 5.7 shows that, for both 1961 and 1966 freshmen, a larger proportion of men are willing to incur over $2,000 in debts for education. Indeed, 36 percent of the 1961 freshmen men and 22 percent of the 1961 freshmen women were willing to incur such debts, whereas 47 percent of the 1966 freshmen men and only 29 percent of the 1966 freshmen women were willing to incur debts that size. These figures, for those enrolled for advanced study, are confirmed in Table 5.8 where 12 percent of the men and 9 percent of the women incurred $2,000 in debts while undergraduates, and 13 percent of the men and 6 percent of the women incurred over $2,000 while graduate students. Although more women than men have loans, they are probably borrowing smaller amounts at a time.

Tables 5.9 and 5.10 reveal that a larger proportion of women rely on personal or family resources to finance education; 38 percent of the men and 46 percent of the women used these resources in their first year of graduate study. This somewhat balances the willingness of men to rely on loans. A large proportion of men attend graduate school with GI benefits. If one could expect men and women to finance graduate school with similar ease, women would have to receive more funds from sources other than GI benefits, since they receive far less from this source. That men do have access to this source supports the conclusion that it is more difficult for women to finance graduate education.

TABLE 5.7

Maximum Debt 1961 and 1966 Freshmen Were Willing to Incur for Graduate Education, by Sex, 1971 (percentages)

Maximum Debt	1961 Freshmen			1966 Freshmen		
	Total (N = 269,608)	Men (N = 174,227)	Women (N = 95,381)	Total (N = 298,328)	Men (N = 183,082)	Women (N = 115,246)
None	45	42	52	35	33	39
Less than $500	5	4	7	5	4	7
$500–999	6	6	6	7	5	9
$1,000–1,999	12	12	13	13	11	14
$2,000–3,999	12	13	11	16	16	17
$4,000–5,999	9	10	6	12	14	8
$6,000–9,999	5	6	3	6	8	3
$10,000–13,999	3	4	1	3	5	1
$14,000 or more	2	3	1	3	4	1
Total	100	100	100	100	100	100

Source: Elaine H. El-Khawa and Ann S. Bisconti, Five and Ten Years After College Entry (Washington, D.C.: American Council on Education, 1974), p. 138.

TABLE 5.8

Debt Incurred for Undergraduate and Graduate Study, by Sex, 1971 Responses of 1961 Freshmen
(percentages)

Debt	Total	Men	Women
Loan for undergraduate study			
None	64	62	68
Less than $500	7	7	6
$500-999	7	8	6
$1,000-1,999	12	12	11
$2,000-3,999	7	8	7
$4,000 or more	3	4	2
Total	100	100	100
N	310,332	194,461	115,871
Loan for graduate study			
None	71	66	80
Less than $500	5	5	4
$500-999	5	6	5
$1,000-1,999	8	10	6
$2,000-3,999	6	7	3
$4,000 or more	5	6	3
Total	100	100	100
N	290,882	185,942	104,941

Source: Elaine H. El-Khawa and Ann S. Bisconti, Five and Ten Years After College Entry (Washington, D.C.: American Council on Education, 1974), p. 134.

TABLE 5.9

Sources of Financial Support for First Year of Advanced Study, by Sex, 1971

Source	Total		Men		Women	
	Number	Percentage	Number	Percentage	Number	Percentage
Fellowships, scholarships, traineeships, etc.						
NSF	5,367	2	4,231	3	1,137	1
NIH, NIMH, PHS	3,777	2	2,187	2	1,590	2
NDEA	6,253	3	4,752	4	1,501	2
Other HEW	2,162	1	862	1	1,300	2
Other U.S. government	5,781	3	4,324	3	1,457	2
State or local government	2,480	1	1,578	1	902	1
School or university	5,935	3	3,630	3	2,305	3
Private foundations, organizations	3,315	2	2,333	2	982	1
Industry or business	2,991	1	2,356	2	635	1
Other fellowships, scholarships	1,651	1	943	1	708	1
Employment						
Faculty appointment	1,325	1	435	*	890	1
Teaching assistantship	11,362	5	8,023	6	3,339	4
Research assistantship	6,136	3	4,592	3	1,543	2
Other part-time during academic year	8,566	4	6,599	5	1,967	2
Other	31,524	14	16,576	12	14,948	18
Other						
Withdrawals from savings, assets	34,775	16	19,326	14	15,449	19
Spouse's earnings or funds	25,829	12	12,942	9	12,887	16
Support from parents or relatives	29,745	14	21,014	15	8,731	11
GI benefits	8,820	4	7,811	6	1,009	1
U.S. government loans	1,640	1	1,311	1	329	*
State or local government loans	774	*	514	*	261	*
Commercial loans (banks, etc.)	2,698	1	1,315	1	1,384	2
Other loans	1,293	1	587	*	707	1
Partial aid from employer (tuition reimbursement or waiver, grants, etc.)	8,932	4	6,134	5	2,798	3
Other	6,343	3	3,167	2	3,175	4
Total	219,476	100	137,542	100	81,934	100

Note: Table shows responses of 1961 freshmen.
*Less than .5.
Source: Elaine H. El-Khawa and Ann S. Bisconti, Five and Ten Years After College Entry (Washington, D.C.: American Council on Education, 1974), p. 127.

TABLE 5.10

All Current Sources of Financial Support for Advanced Study, by Sex, 1971

Source	Total Number (N = 207,208)	Total Percentage	Men Number (N = 20,098)	Men Percentage	Women Number (N = 7,110)	Women Percentage
Fellowships, scholarships, traineeships, etc.						
NSF	567	2	500	2	68	1
NIH, NIMH, PHS	1,626	6	1,000	5	627	9
NDEA	1,209	4	966	5	244	3
Other HEW	397	2	237	1	160	2
Other U.S. government	2,700	10	2,306	12	395	6
State or local government	1,193	4	971	5	222	3
School or university	4,572	17	3,770	19	802	11
Private foundations, organizations	1,108	4	855	4	252	4
Industry or business	657	2	563	3	93	1
Other fellowships, scholarships	551	2	411	2	140	2
Employment						
Faculty appointment	452	2	317	2	135	2
Teaching assistantship	4,373	16	3,756	19	618	9
Research assistantship	4,173	15	3,733	19	440	6
Other part-time during academic year	5,008	18	3,590	18	1,418	20
Other	2,732	10	2,382	12	350	5
Other						
Withdrawals from savings, assets	9,012	33	6,668	33	2,344	33
Spouse's earnings or funds	9,899	36	7,094	35	2,805	40
Support from parents or relatives	3,741	14	2,757	14	984	14
GI benefits	7,008	26	6,348	32	660	9
U.S. government loans	2,140	8	1,741	9	399	6
State or local government loans	919	3	769	4	150	2
Commercial loans (banks, etc.)	1,833	7	1,329	7	504	7
Other loans	1,204	4	1,069	5	135	2
Partial aid from employer (tuition reimbursement or waiver, grants, etc.)	1,423	5	940	5	483	7
Other	1,080	4	722	4	357	5

Note: Table shows responses from 1961 freshmen.
Source: Elaine H. El-Khawa and Ann S. Bisconti, Five and Ten Years After College Entry (Washington, D.C.: American Council on Education, 1974), p. 132.

Apparently, graduate schools provide similar financial opportunities for men and women with resources they control, a first step in financial equity. Since men appear more willing to borrow and clearly have greater access to GI benefits, equal financial opportunity would require that a disproportionate amount of financial aid (other than loans and the GI bill) go to women. But at least institutions have taken the first step toward equalizing their fund distribution.

Data from the survey of graduate deans are in some disagreement with data obtained in 1971 from 1961 freshmen on major sources of financial support (see Tables 5.9 and 5.10). Table 5.9 reports major support during the first year of advanced study, probably awarded sometime in the late 1960s before sensitivity to differential treatment became widespread. At that time, 22 percent of the men and only 16 percent of the women received fellowships, scholarships, and traineeships. However, only 3 percent of the men received research assistantships in their first year, compared with 2 percent of the women, a difference smaller than that revealed in the more recent survey. Almost the same number of men and women had other types of employment during their first year of graduate study. Moreover, a larger proportion of women relied on their own savings, spouses' earnings, or support from parents or relatives. Few students were dependent on loans of any kind.

Table 5.10 discusses current sources of financial support for advanced study; that is, support during the 1971 academic year, much nearer in time to the survey of graduate deans. In this case, 58 percent of the men and only 42 percent of the women were receiving fellowships, scholarships, and traineeships. The differences by sex in awarding research assistantships confirms data from the deans' survey: 19 percent of the men but only 6 percent of the women held research positions. Moreover, at this later time (compared with first-year financial information), both men and women relied equally on other sources to finance their studies, such as personal savings, spouses' earnings, or support from parents and relatives. The 1961 freshmen still in graduate school in 1971 had probably used up most institutional or government support. Awards are not made to students in their fifth year of graduate work.

To determine relationships between financial aid awards and institutional and student characteristics, a series of regressions was run to explain differences among institutions in proportions of men and women receiving various awards, the differences between the proportions of men and women receiving certain types of awards, and differences in dollar values. Interinstitutional differences were assessed by such factors as institutional affluence, Roose-Andersen ratings, the proportion of doctoral work in the natural sciences, enrollment, and the proportion of women faculty. In addition, several student control variables were inserted: average graduate record examination (GRE) scores of applicants, the proportion of graduates married, and the proportion of women graduates. These data are available for less than 50 institutions, so the validity of the regressions must not be overemphasized. No regression tables are presented but the more pertinent results are summarized.

Institutional affluence had surprisingly little effect on any dependent variable, except that wealthier institutions tended to provide larger stipends for teaching assistantships. With nonservice awards, a negative relationship existed between total enrollment and the proportion of each sex receiving an award. A negative relationship also existed between the proportion of women with teaching assistantships and total enrollment.

Confirming an earlier hypothesis about more available aid in the natural sciences, a significantly positive relationship existed between the proportion of women receiving nonservice awards and the proportion of Ph.D.'s with degrees in the natural sciences. Also, the relationship between the proportion of doctorates in the natural sciences and the value of awards for research and teaching assistantships to women was positive. Hence, in institutions emphasizing the natural sciences, women received more nonservice awards or were paid more when awards required work. Those institutions with a larger proportion of women on the faculty had the smallest proportion of women with nonservice awards. Institutions with the most women faculty had the smallest proportion of men and women with research assistantships. The relationship between the proportion of women faculty and the value of research assistantships was also negative. These relationships are probably due to women faculty clustering in such fields as humanities, where the fewest funds are available.

Institutions with the best students, as measured by average GRE scores, have the largest proportion of both men and women with nonservice awards. The relationship between the proportion of women receiving both research and teaching assistantships and average GRE scores was negative. Institutions with less able students were more likely to award women research or teaching assistantships, while institutions with higher-quality students were more likely to award women nonservice grants. The relationship between the average GRE score and the dollar value of research and teaching assistantships is positive, implying that better students received better-paying work arrangements.

In the regression analysis the proportion of men or women who are married had few systematic relationships. Generally, a smaller proportion of students of one sex received awards, and those awards were smaller when more students of that sex were married. For example, schools with more married men awarded men lower stipends for their research and teaching assistantships. However, institutions in which a larger proportion of graduate students were married women provided women nonservice stipends with greater value. The proportion of Ph.D.'s awarded to women was never significant in any financial aid variable regression.

These variables explain approximately 50 percent of the inter-institutional differences in the percentage of men and women students with nonservice awards. In assessing the proportion receiving research and teaching assistantships and the value of all types of awards, these variables did not explain anywhere near 50 percent of the variance among institutions. Besides the conclusion that institutions with better students give a larger proportion of them nonservice awards, the major finding concerns the relationship between emphasis on natural sciences, as evidenced by the proportion of Ph.D.'s in the natural sciences and by the proportion of women faculty, and aid available to women. In most cases, significant variables did not have differential effects in explaining financial aid awards for men and women.

Regressions to explain the differences in the proportion of men and women awarded various aid show the same results. Institutions emphasizing natural sciences gave less advantage to men in financial aid awards. Larger institutions favored men less in research and more in teaching assistantships. Where a larger proportion of the women were married, a larger proportion of the research assistantships were made to men. Institutions in which GRE scores for men were better favored men in several kinds of awards. In assessing differences in propensity to award men or women, this study could explain little of the interinstitutional difference.

What can one conclude from the evidence presented here? First, any conclusions must be tempered by the finding that reports from graduate deans reveal less discrimination in financial aid than reports from students. However, the observations here are based on data from the deans which are more recent than those from students and, clearly, discrimination by sex has declined each year. Be that as it may, the share of awards to each sex, as a proportion of applicants, is at least equal, with the successful application rate of women slightly higher than that of men. Despite this, differences by field do appear, with women receiving a disproportionately large number of financial aid awards compared with their enrollment in the physical sciences, mathematics, and engineering, and fewer awards, given enrollment, in the life and social sciences. Overall, women receive proportionately less financial aid than men (according to the follow-up of 1961 freshmen), a not inconsistent finding, since a much larger proportion of women are enrolled in life and social sciences, and arts and humanities (the latter group is not included in the statistics in Table 4.8). It is in precisely those fields where women's enrollments are smallest that financial aid is most available. Institutions in general should be commended for their equal treatment of the sexes in distributing money under institutional control.

However, women consistently receive fewer research assistantships and a larger share of teaching assistantships and other service awards. The sparse data do not confirm the generally held hypothesis that the dollar value of awards to men is greater.

Although a few more women take loans, these loans are smaller. And, of course, men benefit much more than women from the GI bill.

Since women are less likely to take large loans and men have greater access to the GI bill, equal distribution of other student aid will not result in equal ability to finance education. To make financing graduate work as easy for women as for men would necessitate allocating service and nonservice awards disproportionately in favor of women. This would be asking a great deal of an institution.

6

Those who charge blatant, malevolent discrimination by the graduate institutions in the United States apparently are basing their accusations on weak evidence. Although some differential treatment of men and women students seeking the Ph.D. degree exists, differences are not as great as certain experiences of individual students imply. However, covert forces (such as attitudes of faculty toward women students), which are difficult to document with empirical data, may be at work rather than overt prejudice.

This study has attempted to produce data on institutions and students that are trustworthy and sufficiently detailed and representative to indicate what discrimination graduate students face because of sex. In most cases, the data are average values for students of each sex in specific institutions. Future research must include large-scale efforts to collect more data on individuals' experiences with applications, acceptances, enrollment, aid, time in graduate school, and more. Also needed are data on behavior in individual departments, since this study was restricted to overall institutional behavior with crude adjustments for field mixes of different graduate schools. It is possible that looking at the data by individual departments would point up instances of discrimination that have heretofore been ignored in analyses of overall institutional behavior.

However, the data presented are more than adequate to support the conclusions. More detailed data may some day enable researchers to elaborate on these observations and provide additional insights. But the new information here is sometimes surprising and at times reassuring. The study revealed fewer sex differences than are sometimes alleged. Those working toward equality for members of both sexes should be heartened by the evidence that their efforts appear to be paying off.

In particular, a greater proportion of women than men who apply to graduate school are accepted. Data in Chapter 2 revealed that, despite popular misconceptions, women applicants to graduate school are not significantly superior to men applicants, if one evaluates student quality by graduate record examination (GRE) scores. However, college grades of women applicants are higher than those of men. Evidently, greater proportions of women are admitted where the GRE is a less important consideration in the admissions process. If discrimination in admissions exists, it is concentrated in the most elite institutions. Some evidence also suggests that women are more conservative in selecting institutions to which they apply (or their self-esteem is lower and so they apply to lower-quality institutions). This conservatism might be due, in part, to recognition or belief that the probability of acceptance or of a financial aid award is lower at some institutions. Decision making by admissions committees appears somewhat different for men and women, but the process apparently does not hurt women's chances for acceptance.

This study has attempted to diffuse some of the myths about the inadvisability of educating women. Some argue that to encourage women to attend graduate school for a doctorate is wasteful, because other responsibilities, primarily toward family, will force them to spend more years and use more resources than men to obtain the degree. That women are older at the time they receive the doctorate is due to their delay in entering graduate school, rather than to more time spent in school. In terms of years of study for the doctorate, women do not take longer than men. All students regardless of sex tend to complete the doctorate faster in the hard sciences, where there are fewer women.

On the one hand, this finding implies that outside responsibilities are not costing society more per degree for women doctorates. On the other hand, it implies that some barriers allegedly imposed by the institutions, faculty, administrators, and so forth are not as great as has been thought. If women are being hindered in their pursuit of the doctorate, they probably would spend more years getting it. Of course, since the data refer only to completers, little is known about the barriers that faced the women who dropped out.

Apparently, women do not move from institution to institution for their graduate work any more frequently than men. Some argue that women must follow their husbands around the country, so they will attend more graduate schools before receiving their Ph.D.'s. It does appear, however, that in selecting institutions, women are not as mobile, do not move out of their home state, and concentrate in urban areas more often than men. Marriage appears to stabilize women rather than cause them to move excessively.

In terms of financial aid, some differences exist between the sexes. Although approximately equal proportions of men and women students receive financial aid, more men receive research assistantships and more women teaching assistantships. This distribution tends to confirm an oft-held belief that men professors are more inclined to work with men than with women students. Since research assistantships

appear to be an important factor in professional development, men benefit more than women. However, women do tend to concentrate in fields
where research assistantships are rare. In the hard sciences, women
who apply for assistance do better in overall aid than men, but they
still receive a relatively small share of research assistantships. Few
women are enrolled in or graduate from hard science fields compared
with the number of women in life sciences, social sciences, and arts
and humanities. It would be instructive to have data on the share of
research assistantships going to women in such fields as psychology,
where there are both many women and a significant number of research
awards. However, this study did not have such data.

     No evidence was uncovered of any significant difference in the
size of stipends for men and women; the evidence in this study show-
ing slight advantages for men is quite weak, since the data cover only
50 institutions. Women appear to receive their fair share of financial
aid (number of awards), whether this fair share is defined in terms of
numbers that enroll or numbers that apply. Much of the observed disadvantage of women is based on different distribution of men and women
among fields, since less aid is available in fields where women tend
to enroll.

     Apparently, more men than women are willing to incur debts by
taking out loans. Men also have an additional source of aid through
the GI bill. If these two means of financing education are added to
the otherwise relatively equal arrangements for men and women in terms
of institutional, government, and other types of support, they tip the
balance in favor of men.

     A larger proportion of women than men say they did not enroll in
their first-choice institution because they received better financial aid
offers from less preferred institutions. However, fewer women than
men enroll in non-first choice institutions. No analysis was made of
award offers to members of each sex by institutional quality, but one
can infer that men might be favored for financial aid at the best institutions—those that would normally be the first choice of all students.

     One wonders to what extent the universities are responsible for
the different experiences of men and women. Perhaps more effort could
be made to recruit women into fields where they have not traditionally
enrolled. If such an effort were made, the quality of women students
would probably change in the hard sciences, where now only top-
quality women enter. Some of the newly recruited women would probably
be equal to the exceptional women currently enrolled in the hard sciences,
but to achieve equality, opportunities must be made available to a
broader spectrum of able women, as they are now to a broader spectrum
of men. This change might lead to more equal distribution of financial
aid between men and women, where now the few women are favored
because they are so exceptional. That men are receiving more aid in
the so-called "feminine" fields is probably due to the greater variance
in the quality of women there. Also, these fields may be attempting to

attract more men to increase their perceived status. However, if men are favored in these fields, institutions might take some steps to redress this imbalance. Moreover, explicit attempts to award women more research than teaching assistantships might be useful.

Efforts to encourage women to enter the "hard" sciences must include counseling at the high school and undergraduate level to attract women to and prepare them for the prerequisite courses. To start solving the problem at a level as advanced as graduate school is difficult. However, most differences in financial aid patterns and in time required to obtain the degree are related to differences in the distribution of men and women by field.

A relatively small but growing proportion of doctorates are awarded to women (under 20 percent in 1973), implying that graduate schools should make a greater effort to recruit, financially support, and encourage women students. However, unless women meet the graduate school's prerequisites, particularly the requirements of the best schools, it is impossible for the graduate schools to attract qualified women—graduate schools cannot attract what is not there. Hence, one must advocate greater consciousness in high school and college of the desirability of women obtaining advanced degrees.

The graduate schools cannot be blamed for a socialization and conditioning process that begins in the United States virtually at birth. Of course, they can be blamed for not taking affirmative steps to counteract its effects. Facilitating mechanisms certainly could be installed in the universities: day-care centers, proper medical care, special class schedules to assist women with families, wider credit transferability, reduced residence requirements, and acceptance of part-time students, perhaps even awards of financial aid for part-time study. But these steps are suggested too often without additional thought. If day-care centers are desirable and in demand, why cannot some private individual establish one or more near major university centers? Presumably, if the benefits were worth the cost, many potential graduate women would make use of them. The cost of day-care facilities should be included in needs criteria for financial aid for women (and for men!). But could it be that the families involved decide that the benefits of graduate education for women are less than the benefits to children of having their mother at home? Once again the question arises whether this attitude, where it exists, comes from a well-thought-out cost/benefit analysis by the family, or whether it is a residual from generations of societal customs.

Similarly, why does the family situation place almost all the burden on women? Although this societal norm is long standing, apparently a tendency is developing toward sharing family responsibilities between husband and wife. That women in this society have tended to carry the burden may not be blamed on graduate institutions. Similar cases might be made for the small number of women who receive the doctorate. Certainly, society conditions women to seek other paths.

However, some women, who have not been brainwashed by society, of their own free will might choose other paths more frequently than their masculine peers. One cannot lay too much blame on the graduate schools, although one can produce lists of steps they might take to make graduate education easier for women.

One reason for this study was to question the necessity and value of affirmative action programs in the graduate schools. Unfortunately, time-series data are not available to observe changes in sex differences in graduate schools over, perhaps, the last ten years. However, the snapshots of the years 1972 to 1974 promote confidence that women are not doing too badly now. Whether this finding can be attributed to affirmative action legislation or whether it merely reflects changing attitudes in society is undetermined. Discrimination by graduate schools in faculty hiring, promotion, pay, and the like has not been discussed here. Possibly legislation is necessary to stimulate equality at the postgraduate level. A more positive attitude toward women faculty in hiring, promotion, and salary could provide women students with more appropriate role models and, with nonsexist counseling in the high schools and colleges, might attract more women students to an institution. However, even though some differential treatment exists, for whatever reasons, women graduate students, at this time in history, are not a totally underprivileged minority.

At least two reasons emerge for looking at the degree of sexism in graduate school catalogues. First, these documents are really the only significant, generally available "consumer information" produced by institutions. Although general impressions of institutional quality, available aid, and advice from undergraduate teachers probably determine the initial interest of students, the catalogues may give more concrete impressions to potential applicants, playing a subtle role in the decision of whether or not to apply to a particular graduate school.

Second, the catalogues reveal the degree of explicit institutional sensitivity toward sex differences. An institution that is not careful to take sexism out of its catalogues probably lacks awareness of other factors relative to discrimination against women graduate students.

Some 213 graduate school catalogues were examined for their indirect appeal to women through use of masculine and feminine pronouns, their direct appeal through civil rights statements, and for the sex of people in photographs.

Some educators have suggested that more women students could be recruited for technical and professional programs by such techniques as eliminating masculine pronouns and using pictures of women in publicity.

METHOD

A mimeographed letter requesting a current (1973-74) graduate catalogue was sent to each institution on the Council of Graduate Schools or the National Academy of Science lists of graduate degree-granting institutions. Requests were sent to institutions with master's programs and to graduate subdivisions (such as Yale University, Graduate School of Forestry). The master's-only institutions were later excluded from the survey and the responses of subdivisions combined with the main graduate schools' statistics. Eventually, the catalogue analysis was limited to the 239 doctorate-granting institutions, of which 213 sent a graduate catalogue. If a catalogue contained information on both the graduate and undergraduate programs, only the graduate section was studied (with the exception of a direct appeal statement in the introduction).

RESULTS

Catalogues classified as making a direct appeal to women did one or more of the following:

1. Made a civil rights compliance statement that included the word sex.
2. Used words "men and women" in describing the student body.
3. Used term "coeducational" to describe the institution.

Some 37 percent of the catalogues included at least one of the above; 63 percent included none of the above.

The institutions that made an appeal to women usually did so in the first few pages of the catalogue. The appeal was frequently a standard sentence on civil rights compliance that included the word "sex," or a statement such as "we encourage applications from qualified men and women." In at least a dozen catalogues, civil rights statements appeared that excluded the word "sex." No catalogue made a specific statement such as "We want women students." (Texas Women's University said it accepted men only to comply with civil rights laws and only in majors with federal dealings.)

In regard to pronoun reference, schools were classified as follows:

1. M—masculine pronouns only.
2. M and F—masculine and feminine pronouns together (he/she or his and her).
3. N (neutral or neither sex used)—pronouns that could be applied to either sex (their, your)

If the words he, his, or him were used five times, the institution was listed as a user of masculine pronouns. This designation was rather arbitrary, and in some instances it could be conferred after one paragraph.

Approximately 82.63 percent (176) used M only; 4.23 percent (9) used M and F; 11.27 percent (24) used N; and 1.88 percent (4) used combinations.

In regard to photographs, categories included:

1. None—no pictures or only pictures of buildings, landscapes.
2. Both—pictures of both men and women.
3. Men—pictures of men only.

Of the catalogues, 52.58 percent (112) had no pictures or only pictures of buildings; 43.19 percent (92) had both men and women in pictures; and 4.23 percent (9) had only men in pictures.

111

Institutions that pictured only men included: California Institute of Technology, City University of New York, Duke University, Institute of Paper Technology, U.S. Naval Postgraduate School, Texas A and M University, University of Missouri, Rolla, University of South Dakota, University of Texas, Arlington.

Seven of these nine institutions also used only masculine pronouns and did not make an appeal to women.

In regard to women's studies, only 1.4 percent (3) of the schools had a graduate program in women's studies listed in the catalogue: University of South Florida, University of Maryland, Baltimore County, George Washington University.

The balance—98.6 percent (210)—listed no women's studies.

Of the 213 catalogues, 4.7 percent (10) demonstrated no favoritism, used F pronouns, made an appeal to women, and did not use only men in photographs: Georgia State University, Indiana State University, Middlebury College, Smith College, Texas Women's University (direct appeal to men), University of Michigan, University of North Dakota, University of Oregon, South Dakota School of Technology.

SIGNIFICANCE

Findings of the catalogue analysis appear to indicate unconscious rather than conscious attempts to exclude women. However, the present picture is discouraging.

A review of institutional reports on the status of women faculty and graduate students revealed that several reports include recommendations to change the references in institutional documents to include both masculine and feminine nouns and photographs of men and women faculty and students. One such institution was City University of New York, which in this analysis had only photographs of men. A report to the chancellor recommended that the university amend its bylaws to include a clear statement prohibiting sex discrimination in employment, admissions, and publications.

There seems to be a growing awareness of the subtle effect of precluding the mention and appearance of women in college catalogues. A survey of 1974-75 catalogues might find women better represented.

Concern about the possibility of discrimination on college campuses has prompted numerous reports by individual institutions. A survey of 33 reports was conducted to determine how different institutions perceive discrimination and what recommendations they make to eliminate injustice. All reports are from doctorate-granting institutions; investigations ranged from faculty salaries to undergraduate admissions. Because the documents were written by individuals or committees for different purposes, their focus and tone vary (see Table A.1 for a breakdown of individual reports).

The majority of the reports were written by ad hoc committees appointed to investigate discrimination. About half these committees were composed entirely of women; the balance contained men. Faculty members almost always participated in the investigations, and at least half the groups included students. Only one surveyed report originated in a student group.

The high proportion of faculty members on investigative committees reflects the major target of study: the representation and treatment of women in faculty and administrative ranks. Twenty studies dealt with issues relevant to graduate students, suggesting interrelated treatment of women graduate students and faculty. Fewer studies addressed the conditions of staff members (11) and undergraduate students (14). In an ambitious report of the City University of New York's 20 campuses, the Chancellor's Advisory Committee on the Status of Women "began its work with two hypotheses: first, that discrimination against women would likely be found within the CUNY system and second, that the operating policies and practices of CUNY affected all women in the system" (p. 4). Although many investigators acknowledged the need to study women in all positions, lack of time, staff, or financing caused them to focus on the status of faculty women.

The motivation to set up investigative committees most frequently came from administrators, such as presidents, chancellors, or deans. Seven committees were established on the recommendation of faculty bodies. Chapters of the American Association of University Professors requested four of the studies. At eight of the institutions, concerned individuals organized themselves to study discrimination. One such group, representing the associated students at the University of Washington, instigated its study because of "the troubling recognition that the status of women in American academic institutions has actually deteriorated in the last four decades" (p. 2). The group at the University of Washington, as at many institutions, was familiar with reports written by other campus groups and felt a need "to do the same in hopes of identifying problems and facilitating change" (p. 2).

113

The researchers at different institutions encountered various receptions in their attempts to acquire institutional data. Some reports gratefully credited the helpfulness of university offices, while others pointed out the inadequacy of the institution's record-keeping systems. One committee of women at the University of Pittsburgh thought its efforts were blocked by the administration. In their words, "The University . . . displayed an exemplary ability to stall, issue high-sounding policy statements which signify nothing, and cloud true issues with charges that we do not represent the women of the university" (p. 2). Most researchers gathered data from many sources: institutional data banks, personnel files, budget and payroll reports, and college catalogues. More than one-third of the investigations included surveys of faculty and/or students that utilized questionnaires. Nine reports incorporated information acquired through personal interviews. Public hearings were held by five institutions; CUNY published its testimony in a condensed version, Public Hearings Testimony: An Edited Summary and Evaluation, in October 1972.

The general outlook for women on college campuses as presented in the majority of reports appears poor. With the exception of Indiana State University, which reported favorable employment opportunities for women faculty, the institutions outlined conditions that need attention. Yale reported that "a genuine problem does, in fact, exist. As the situation now stands, an unacceptably high fraction of advanced students at Yale do not reach the professional fulfillment to which their training ought to entitle them" (p. 2). Likewise, through their study, the commissioners at Carnegie-Mellon University perceived the institution as "a place where women do not enjoy full equity with men" (p. 10). CUNY concluded that "women as a group are not treated equitably throughout the CUNY system. Moreover, CUNY is fraught with sex typing of educational and occupational categories and is therefore unable to provide a full range of opportunities to individuals regardless of sex" (p. 6).

The most frequently voiced finding was that women are inadequately represented in prestige positions. "The Higher, the Fewer" is the title of the University of Michigan report, which succinctly states the problem. The percentage of women employed as professors and assistant or associate professors ranges from 28.5 percent at the University of Kansas to 3 percent at Yale. The University of Chicago, which reported that women constituted 7.3 percent of the regular teaching faculty in spring 1969 (excluding 7 percent of the Department of Physical Education), made a distinction between "elite" universities and other universities. "The overall figure is considerably below the average for all universities, but it compares favorably, so far as we have been able to ascertain, with those universities which, like the University of Chicago, view themselves as 'elite.' These 'elite' universities generally have smaller numbers of women on their faculties than do other universities" (p. 1). Certain institutions in small towns or rural areas pointed out the difficulty of attracting women to their faculties.

The small number of women in faculty positions results in what Princeton referred to as "a total lack of adequate role models" for graduate and undergraduate students. Harvard University mentioned a related problem: "The absence of women in the upper ranks of the regular faculty has created among female members a general feeling of isolation. Women faculty members voice exactly the same sense of being intruders in a male institution that Radcliffe students express about their participation in Harvard College" (p. 7).

However, women who do achieve a position of status in the "elite" institutions receive a salary comparable to that of men. At Harvard, the committee "discovered no case of a woman in a regular faculty appointment who is paid less than her male counterpart" (p. 5). Eighteen reports found unexplainable discrepancies between men's and women's salaries. Women have difficulty receiving promotions, according to 21 reports, and obtaining tenure, according to 10 reports. Fourteen reports discussed university policies that disadvantage women faculty. Although most institutions have relaxed nepotism rules, policy statements in faculty handbooks can be ambiguous and their interpretation may be left to individual departments. Some institutions do not have maternity leaves for women or equal medical and insurance benefits for faculty men and women. Some reports mentioned the desirability of part-time assignments for interested full-time faculty, an option rarely permitted.

Findings of unequal treatment of men and women graduate students were not clearcut. Ten of the nineteen institutions that investigated admissions thought their findings inconclusive. In some instances, conflicting records were received from different offices. Some reports commented that the numbers of men and women accepted do not indicate discriminatory trends unless the numbers of applicants and their qualifications are also considered. The University of North Dakota reported that "while some departments may be collecting data to compare the characteristics of applicants with admitted students, the Graduate School does not have such data" (p. 3). An obvious need for this information exists at most institutions. Only three reports claimed that their institution's admissions appeared unequal, and this was due in part to quota systems. Six investigations concluded that discrimination in admissions does not occur. Their judgments were based on evidence that an equal or greater proportion of women who apply are accepted, a system of analysis that does not consider qualifications.

In assessing whether fellowship and scholarship money is fairly distributed, investigators again ran into difficulties obtaining meaningful data. Five reports explained that a definitive statement about the allotment of financial aid was not possible. Six reports stated that money did not appear to be granted equally to men and women but thought factors other than discrimination could be accountable. Only one institution, the University of North Dakota, contended that financial aid figures demonstrate equal treatment of men and women. Some institutions that surveyed students found that sources of support vary by sex, but this finding does not necessarily illustrate unfair treatment by the institution. In some cases, women receive an equal proportion of awards but smaller amounts of money. Some institutions explained that women usually apply for scholarships in such fields as humanities, where less financial aid is available. Certain institutions, such as Harvard, recently abandoned policies disallowing two married students to receive financial support.

Related to financial aid is the question of whether men and women have equal access to on-campus employment as teaching or research assistants. Only four reports discussed this issue; three concluded that women are disadvantaged. Women also seem to receive fewer post-graduation jobs through departmental ties or career placement centers. Ohio University found that "a higher percentage of men than of women students are being placed successfully in University and off-campus jobs by the Office of Student Financial Aids. Men tend to find traditional 'male' jobs, while women tend to find traditional 'female' jobs" (p. vi). Among problems related to women's job searches are lack of publicity for job openings, requests by employers for men interviewees, and complaints by women about discriminatory hiring. The Carnegie-Mellon report noted that "more women than men use the Bureau of Placement, but a smaller proportion of women are successfully placed in jobs. Although it is undoubtedly true that it is more difficult to place women students in good jobs, given the sex bias of many employers, the Commission felt that the existence of such external prejudice should motivate the Bureau of Placements to take extraordinary measures to assist women students and alumnae who are seeking jobs or need job counseling" (p. 3).

The consensus of virtually every institution that investigated the circumstances of women graduate students was that campus environments do not adequately provide for women's needs. The lack of child-care facilities and the difficulty of arranging part-time studies were mentioned frequently. At some institutions, the monetary allowance for men's athletics far exceeds that for women. Housing is often more expensive for single women, and married student housing has only become available in the last few years to women on some campuses, such as the University of Washington. Women at Ohio University have been prevented from joining the school's marching band, "which is most clearly identified with school pride" (p. vii).

Closely linked with inadequate provisions for women is a general campus atmosphere that often discourages women students. A survey by the University of Chicago revealed "an underlying set of attitudes in both faculty and students that women are not receiving their full share of rewards and encouragement on this campus" (p. 60). Similarly, the University of South Florida stated that "a continuing question among those who study the status of University women is whether or not women are discouraged by counselors and professors as they seek advanced degrees; and the consensus is that they are" (p. 9). The Yale committee believed that the university's reputation of inhospitality to women is firmly entrenched, even off campus. "Yale obviously has a 'male chauvinist' image. It is considered to be a school dominated by men of Old Blue tradition where women are tolerated only. Obviously this is an image which we will find very difficult to shake off. Whether or not Yale is 'male chauvinist' or has been in the recent past, positive steps are needed in order to change this view that others have of us."

Yale's primary recommendation for improvement, and that of many other institutions, is to hire more faculty women. At one open hearing at Harvard, President Mary Bunting of Radcliffe urged that more women be hired. In her opinion, "a great many people on the faculty haven't had the experience of working with able women on a professionally equal level for a great many years . . . and this has had some very unfortunate effects" (p. 18). Harvard proposes to establish as a rough guideline that "the Harvard Faculty of Arts and Sciences strive to achieve a percentage of women in its tenured ranks equal to the percentage of women receiving PhD's from Harvard ten years ago (9.6% in 1959-60) and a percentage of women in the non-tenured ranks equal to the percentage of women receiving PhD's today (19% in 1968-69)" (pp. 32-33). It is understandable that Ivy League schools where coeducation has only recently been established, face difficulties in accommodating women. Affirmative action guidelines are requesting that all institutions with government contracts make reasonable efforts to eliminate the inequities that have resulted in the past.

In their recommendations, most institutions requested that a continuing post or committee be founded to perpetuate research in women's treatment and to process grievances. The person or group would be charged with implementing policies that counteract existing inequalities. These institutions hope that women will hold positions of authority and make decisions beneficial to women faculty and students. These decisions should concern salary equalization, recruitment and advancement of faculty women, more accurate and publicized records of faculty and student data, and the special needs of women of all ages. Improving conditions for women will inadvertently improve the circumstances of men, too.

The various reports generally agreed that discrimination may be unintentional. The University of Chicago concluded that

TABLE B.1

Areas of Investigation

	Faculty (employees)					Policies (maternity leave nepotism)
Institution	Hiring	Representation	Rank	Salary	Tenure	
Bowling Green	+	+	+	+	+	
Brown	+	+	+	−		+
Carnegie-Mellon		+	+	+		
Case Western Reserve	+	+	+	+		+
City Univ. of New York	+	+	+	+	−	+
Columbia Univ.		+	+	+	+	+
Cornell						
Cornell		+	+		+	+
Harvard	+	+	+	0	+	+
Indiana State Univ.	0	0	0	0		0
Michigan State Univ.		+		+	+	
Ohio Univ.	+	+	+	+		+
Princeton		+	+	+		
Rockefeller Univ.				+		
Stanford		+	+		+	
Univ. of Akron				+		
Univ. of California (8 campuses)						
Univ. of California, Berkeley		+	+		+	+
Univ. of Chicago		+	+	−	0	
Univ. of Delaware		+	+	+	+	+
Univ. of Kansas						
Univ. of Maryland		+	+		+	
Univ. of Minnesota	+	+	+	+	0	+
Univ. of Minnesota				+		
Univ. of Michigan		+				
Univ. of North Dakota		+		+		
Univ. of Oregon	+	+	+	+		
Univ. of Pennsylvania		+	+	0		+
Univ. of Pittsburgh	+	+	+	+		+
Univ. of South Florida	+	+	+	+		+
Univ. of Washington						
Univ. of Wisconsin			+	+		
Yale		+			+	+

*Data not available.

Key: + = Discrimination exists.
     − = Discrimination does not exist.
     0 = Insufficient data to answer.
     A = − (undergraduate)
     B = + (graduate)

Admissions	Financial Aid	Teaching and Research Positions	Job Placements	Inflexible or Unwelcoming Environment	Institutional Facilities (housing, counseling, medical services, day care)
Students					
0	0	+		+	
0	0		+	+	+
0					
A	A		+	+	+
	B				
+	+			+	+
-					+
0	0	0	+	+	+
0	+				
	*		+	+	+
+					+
0				+	

did not draw conclusions from data

Admissions	Financial Aid	Teaching and Research Positions	Job Placements	Inflexible or Unwelcoming Environment	Institutional Facilities
0	0	+	+	+	+
-	+			+	+
0					
0	0				
					+
-	+		+	+	+
-	-		-		
+	+		+	+	
-	+	+	-	+	-
0			+	+	

(continued)

TABLE B.1 (continued)

		Groups Studied			
Institution	Faculty	Administration	Staff	Graduate Students	Undergraduate Students
Bowling Green	✓			✓	✓
Brown	✓	✓	✓	✓	✓
Carnegie-Mellon	✓	✓	✓	✓	
Case Western-Reserve	✓				
City Univ. of New York (20 campuses)	✓	✓		✓	✓
Columbia	✓		✓	✓	✓
Cornell	✓				✓
Cornell	✓	✓	✓	✓	
Harvard	✓	✓	✓	✓	✓
Indiana State Univ.	✓	✓	✓	✓	✓
Michigan State Univ.	✓		✓		✓
Ohio Univ.	✓			✓	
Princeton					✓
Rockefeller Univ.					
Stanford	✓			✓	
Univ. of Akron	✓	✓		✓	
Univ. of California (8 campuses)	✓			✓	
Univ. of California, Berkeley	✓			✓	
Univ. of Chicago	✓			✓	
Univ. of Delaware	✓		✓		✓
Univ. of Kansas	✓				
Univ. of Maryland	✓				✓
Univ. of Minnesota	✓				
Univ. of Minnesota	✓	✓		✓	
Univ. of Michigan	✓			✓	✓
Univ. of North Dakota	✓	✓	✓		✓
Univ. of Oregon		✓	✓		
Univ. of Pennsylvania				✓	
Univ. of Pittsburgh				✓	
Univ. of South Florida					
Univ. of Washington (Part II)	✓			✓	✓
Univ. of Wisconsin (16 campuses)	✓				
Yale					

(continued)

120

TABLE B.1 (continued)

Institution	Registrar	Personnel Files	Budget Reports	Payroll Records	University Data Files or Departmental Records	Public Hearings	Interviews	Questionnaires or Letters of Inquiry	Catalogues	Personal Observations
Bowling Green		√						√		
Brown		√							√	
Carnegie-Mellon		√	√			√	√			
Case Western Reserve		√		√		√	√			
City Univ. of New York (20 campuses)							√			
Columbia										√
Cornell										
Cornell										
Harvard	√				√		√	√		
Indiana State Univ.		√				√	√			
Michigan State Univ.					√		√		√	
Ohio Univ.									√	
Princeton										
Rockefeller Univ.										
Stanford					√			√		
Univ. of Akron										
Univ. of California (8 campuses)										
Univ. of California, Berkeley					√					
Univ. of Chicago		√			√	√	√	√	√	
Univ. of Delaware					√		√		√	
Univ. of Kansas					√					
Univ. of Maryland				√	√					
Univ. of Minnesota					√					
Univ. of Minnesota					√					
Univ. of Michigan					√					
Univ. of North Dakota					√			√	√	
Univ. of Oregon	√		√		√			√	√	
Univ. of Pennsylvania		√		√				√		
Univ. of Pittsburgh		√	√	√				√	√	
Univ. of South Florida										
Univ. of Washington (Part II)					√					
Univ. of Wisconsin (16 campuses)					√			√		
Yale					√					

(continued)

TABLE B.1 (continued)

Institution	Publication Date	Individual: Female	Individual: Male	Committee: Female	Committee: Male	Faculty/Administrator	Student(s)	Office of Institutional Research or Central Planning
Bowling Green	1971			✓		✓	✓	
Brown	1970			✓		✓	✓	
Carnegie–Mellon	1971			✓	✓	✓		
Case Western Reserve	1973			✓	✓	✓		
City Univ. of New York (20 campuses)	1972			✓			✓	
Columbia	1969	✓		✓	✓		✓	
Cornell	1970			✓	✓	✓	✓	
Cornell	1974					✓	✓	
Harvard	1971		✓	✓	✓	✓		
Indiana State Univ.	1971			✓	✓			
Michigan State Univ.	1970							✓
Ohio Univ.	1972	✓						
Princeton	1971			✓	✓	✓	✓	
Rockefeller Univ.	1973			✓		✓		
Stanford	1969	✓	✓			✓		
Univ. of Akron	1970			✓	✓			
Univ. of California (8 campuses)	1972			✓	✓	✓		
Univ. of California, Berkeley	1970			✓	✓	✓	✓	
Univ. of Chicago	1970			✓		✓	✓	
Univ. of Delaware	1971			✓	✓	✓	✓	
Univ. of Kansas	1970			✓		✓	✓	
Univ. of Maryland	1969	✓		✓	✓	✓		
Univ. of Minnesota	1971			✓	✓	✓		
Univ. of Minnesota	1970			✓		✓		
Univ. of Michigan	1974			✓	✓	✓		
Univ. of North Dakota	1972			✓				
Univ. of Oregon	1970			✓	✓			
Univ. of Pennsylvania	1971			✓				
Univ. of Pittsburgh	1970			✓				
Univ. of South Florida	1970					✓		
Univ. of Washington (Part II)	1971						✓	
Univ. of Wisconsin (16 campuses)	1971			✓	✓			✓
Yale	1971			✓				

(continued)

Table D.1 (Continued)

Institution	Requested by Administrator(s)	Requested by Faculty or Other Body	Reason for Report		Response to Discrimination Charge (HEW)
			Requested by AAUP	Self-Motivated	
Bowling Green					
Brown		✓			
Carnegie-Mellon	✓✓		✓		
Case Western Reserve	✓				
City Univ. of New York (20 campuses)	✓				
Columbia					
Cornell	✓✓			✓✓	
Cornell					
Harvard	✓			✓	
Indiana State Univ.		Did not state			
Michigan State Univ.	✓				
Ohio Univ.					
Princeton		Did not state			
Rockefeller Univ.		Did not state			
Stanford		Did not state		✓	
Univ. of Akron					
Univ. of California (8 campuses)					
Univ. of California, Berkeley		✓✓		✓✓	
Univ. of Chicago					
Univ. of Delaware		✓			
Univ. of Kansas					
Univ. of Maryland					
Univ. of Minnesota	✓ (did not say who charged)				
Univ. of Minnesota	✓✓				
Univ. of Michigan					
Univ. of North Dakota			✓	✓	
Univ. of Oregon		✓			
Univ. of Pennsylvania		✓	✓		
Univ. of Pittsburgh				✓ (p. 13)	
Univ. of South Florida					✓
Univ. of Washington (Part II)				✓	
Univ. of Wisconsin (16 campuses)					
Yale	✓				

"by and large the problems that can be alleviated by changes in University procedures stem more from faults of omission than of commission, more from lack of awareness than from deliberate acts of discrimination" (p. 57). And Ohio University suggested that "it is true that men are only now becoming concerned about the University's unequal treatment of women, but women must share the blame because they have quietly accepted the back seat for years" (p. 47).

The reports indicate hope for the advancement of women in higher education. As summarized by the University of Michigan, "accurate information regularly disseminated is a powerful instrument of change. Discriminatory structures and behavior thrive in the absence of information but suffer the light of public knowledge" (p. 32).

UNIVERSITY REPORTS REVIEWED

Bowling Green State University. The Status of Women Faculty at Bowling Green State University. Faculty Senate Ad Hoc Committee on the Status of Women, May 1972.

Brown University: L. Lamphere et al. Report of the AAUP Committee on the Employment and Status of Women Faculty and Women Graduate Students at Brown. October 1970.

Carnegie-Mellon University. Summary of the Final Report of the Commission on the Status and Needs of Women at Carnegie-Mellon University. November 1971.

Case Western Reserve University. Report of the President's Advisory Committee on the Status of Women in the University. January 1973.

City University of New York. The Status of Women at the City University of New York: A Report to the Chancellor. Chancellor's Advisory Committee on the Status of Women at the City University of New York. December 1972.

Columbia University. Columbia Women's Liberation: Report from the Committee on Discrimination Against Women Faculty. December 1969.

Columbia University: L. Greenhouse. "Columbia Accused of Bias on Women." New York Times, January 11, 1970.

Cornell University: B. Francis. The Status of Women at Cornell. 1970.

Cornell University. A Commitment to Equality: One Century Later. Ad
Hoc Trustee Committee on the Status of Women. Cornell University, March 1974.

Harvard University. Report of the Committee on the Status of Women in
the Faculty of Arts and Sciences. April 1971.

Indiana State University: W. Hardaway. The Status of Women on the
Faculty of Indiana State University. Winter 1971.

Michigan State University. A Compilation of Data on Faculty at Michigan State University, by Sex, Fall 1973. Office of the Provost
(Institutional Research), July 1974.

Ohio University: J. Price. Report on the Status of Women at Ohio University. April 1972.

Princeton University. A Preliminary Report on the Status of Women at
Princeton University. Task Force on Equal Academic Opportunities,
Central New Jersey Chapter, National Organization for Women,
April 1971.

Rockefeller University: C. M. Leonard. An Inquiry into the Status of
Women in Science: A Report to the Standing Committee on University Affairs. January 1973.

Stanford University: A. E. Siegel and R. G. Carr. "Education of
Women at Stanford University." Study of Education at Stanford 7
(March 1969).

University of Akron: D. D. Van Fleet. Salaries of Males and Females:
A Sample of Conditions at the University of Akron. December
1970.

University of California: R. H. Pearce, H. W. Johnson, and H. W.
Magoun. Women in the Graduate Academic Sector of the University of California. June 1972.

University of California, Berkeley: L. W. Sells. Preliminary Report
on the Status of Graduate Women: University of California,
Berkeley. Graduate Assembly's Committee on the Status of
Women, March 1973.

University of California, Berkeley. Report of the Subcommittee on the
Status of Academic Women on the Berkeley Campus. Committee
on Senate Policy, May 1970.

University of Chicago. Women in the University of Chicago. Committee
on University Women, May 1970.

University of Connecticut. "University of Connecticut Affirmative Action
Plan, Response to HEW Report of Findings, January 2, 1973."
University of Connecticut Chronicle 3, no. 9 (February 9, 1973).

University of Delaware: K. H. Dahl. Report on Women at the University
of Delaware. 1971.

University of Kansas: S. Bocell. Reports of Associated Women Students
Commission on the Status of Women. 1969-70.

University of Maryland: B. Sandler. Sex Discrimination at the University
of Maryland. Women's Equity Action League. Fall 1969.

University of Michigan. The Higher, the Fewer. Committee to Study the
Status of Women in Graduate Education and Later Careers, Executive Board of the Graduate School. March 1974.

University of Minnesota: B. Robinett et al. Report of Subcommittee on
Equal Opportunities for Faculty and Student Women. April 1971.

University of Minnesota. Summary Report: Research on the Status of
Faculty Women, University of Minnesota. Minnesota Planning
and Counseling Center for Women. May 1970.

University of North Dakota. The Status of Women at UND 1971-72.
Committee on the Status of Women in the Profession, Report to
AAUP. April 1972.

University of Oregon: J. Acker et al. The Status of Women at the
University of Oregon. Ad Hoc Committee. 1970.

University of Pennsylvania. Women Faculty in the University of Pennsylvania. Committee on the Status of Women. March 1971.

University of Pennsylvania. A Report on the University of Pennsylvania
Affirmative Action Program. Office of the Provost. April 1973
(revised December 1973).

University of Pittsburgh. Discrimination Against Women at the University of Pittsburgh. University Committee for Women's Rights.
November 1970.

University of South Florida. Proposal for an Affirmative Action Plan for
Women at the University of South Florida. Presidential Committee
for the Status of Women. January 1972.

University of South Florida: M. Mackay. Status of Women Committee: Faculty Report. November 1970.

University of Washington. A Report on the Status of Women at the University of Washington, Part II: Undergraduate and Graduate Students. May 1971.

University of Wisconsin. Final Report on Status of Academic Women—1971. Central University Office of Planning and Analysis. 1971.

Yale University. A Report to the President from the Committee on the Status of Professional Women at Yale. May 1971.

Yale University: E. W. Bakke. "Graduate Education for Women at Yale." Ventures: Magazine of the Yale Graduate School. Fall 1969.

Project on Women

STUDY OF OPPORTUNITIES FOR MALE AND FEMALE GRADUATE STUDENTS

Directed by Lewis C. Solmon, Principal Investigator, Project on Women
With the support of the National Institute of Education

The accompanying letter requests that you assist in this survey of graduate schools.

NOTE: All information is regarded as confidential and will be used for statistical purposes only. It will not be released in any way that will allow your specific institution to be identified.

If questions arise regarding the meaning of any items, please do not hesitate to call collect the Office of the Project on Women—(703) 471-5434 for clarification. Please return completed questionnaire to: Dr. Lewis C. Solmon, Director, Project on Women, Virginia Polytechnic Institute and State University, 12100 Sunset Hills Road, Reston, Virginia 22090.

We hope you can return the questionnaire by October 15, 1973.

Please Do Not Write
In This Space

1
1

Office of the Graduate Dean   Institution _____ (2-7)

2 3 4 5 6 7

1. Fields covered in data provided: (8-16)

8 __ Physical Sciences   13 __ Engineering
9 __ Life Sciences   14 __ Education
10 __ Social Sciences   15 __ Business
11 __ Arts & Humanities   16 __ Other Professional (specify)
12 __ Other (specify) _____

8 9 10 11 12
13 14 15 16

2. Year for which data is reported:

1 __ 1972-73   2 __ Other (specify) _____   (17)

17

128

3. Are you reporting for the whole university?   1 __ Yes   2 __   (18)

   If yes, go to Question 4.

   If no, are you reporting for (check as many as apply):

   __ Main campus   __ Branch campus(es)   __ Off campus programs (including extension)

   (19-21)

APPLICATIONS AND ACCEPTANCES

	NUMBER		AVERAGE GRE SCORES*		
				Total	
				Math & Verbal	
	Male	Female	Male	Female	
4. Number of "New" Applicants for Admission to Degree Programs in Your Graduate School	(22-29)			(30-35)	
5. Number of These Admitted (Accepted) by the University	(36-43)			(44-49)	
6. Number of These Matriculated (Enrolled)	(50-57)			(58-63)	

("New" applicants to your graduate school means students applying to your institution who have not been enrolled previously in your institution (as graduate students) even though they might have attended graduate school elsewhere. Graduate students who apply or enroll later than the fall of a given year, but are in residence for the major portion of the academic year are counted as if they had enrolled in the fall.)

*Are these the GRE scores for all those included in the "Numbers" column?   1 __ Yes   2 __ No   (64)

If no, please indicate number for whom you have scores and the categories into which they fall. (i.e. Do only certain departments require the GRE, are they required only of students with grades below a certain level, etc.?)

_____

_____

CONTINUED ON NEXT PAGE

129

ENROLLMENT

	Male	Female

7. Number of Full-Time on Campus Graduate Enrollment

(Fall 1972-73   1 ___ , or year reporting   2 ___ ___)   (65-69)

a) New enrollments to your institution (should equal totals in Question 6).   ___ (70-73)   ___ (74-77)

b) Returning students . . . .   ___ (8-11)   ___ (12-15)

c) Total enrollment . . . .   ___ (16-20)   ___ (21-25)

|2|

8. Number of Part-Time Graduate Students

a) Attending day-time classes . . . .   ___ (26-28)   ___ (29-31)

b) Attending evening classes only . . . .   ___ (32-34)   ___ (35-37)

(NOTE: THESE STUDENTS WOULD NOT BE INCLUDED IN QUESTION 7 ABOVE)

9. Number of Degrees Awarded to Full-Time Students During the 1972-73 Academic Year (or year reporting)

a) Masters or equivalent (terminal at your institution; i.e. no longer enrolled here) . . . .   ___ (38-40)   ___ (41-43)

b) Masters or equivalent (to students who returned for further study, e.g. PhD) . . . .   ___ (44-46)   ___ (47-49)

c) Doctor of Philosophy . . . .   ___ (50-52)   ___ (53-55)

d) Other doctorates, equivalent to the PhD . . . . .   ___ (56-58)   ___ (59-61)

10. Number of Full-Time Students (excluding those reported in Question 9b) Enrolled in Fall of 1972 Still Matriculated in Fall of 1973 (or in following academic year to that reported in Question 7) . . . .   ___ (62-65)   ___ (66-69)

11. Withdrawals of Full-Time Students between Fall of 1972 and Fall of 1973 Due to:

|3|

a) Less than normal progress (your definition). . . . .   ___ (70-72)   ___ (73-75)

b) Other (e.g. leaves of absence, etc.) . . . . .   ___ (8-10)   ___ (11-13)

TOTAL 9 through 11 (should equal totals in Question 7c) . . .   ___ (14-18)   ___ (19-23)

FINANCIAL AID

Please give financial aid information for full-time students only. If this is not possible, please indicate if your report is for both full-time and part-time students. ___ (24)

	NUMBER		AVERAGE VALUE OF AWARD			
			Direct Stipend		Tuition & Fee Waivers	
	Male	Female	Male	Female	Male	Female
			$	$ (25-46)	$	$ (25-46)

12. Number Receiving Non-Service Awards . . .

   a) Awarded by your institution
     i) Fellowships or scholarships . . .   (47-68) |4
     ii) Traineeships . . .   (8-29)
     iii) Other . . .   (30-51)
   b) Awarded by external (other) sources . . .   (52-73) |5

13. Number Receiving Awards for Service (i.e. other non-repayable aid) . . .   (8-29)

If possible, please provide separate information by checking as many categories as appropriate and providing information for each, as indicated:

   a) ___ Research Assistantships . . .   (30-51)
   b) ___ Teaching Assistantships . . .   (52-73) |6
   c) ___ Other Graduate Assistantships . . .   (8-29)
   d) ___ Instructorships . . .   (30-51)
   e) ___ Other . . .   (52-73) |7

14. Number Receiving Loans from Your Institution . . .   (8-13)

15. Number of Students with GI Bill Benefits . . .   (14-19)

16. Would you be able or provide comparable data for:
   a) Separate fields or groups of fields   1 ___ Yes   2 ___ No   (20)
   b) Other years:
     i) More than 5 years ago   1 ___ Yes   2 ___ No   (21)
     ii) Earlier years but not as far back as 5 years   1 ___ Yes   2 ___ No   (22)
     iii) A later year   1 ___ Yes   2 ___ No   (23)

Date _____ Signature _____ Title _____ (24)

If you are interested in receiving summary data and copies of reports, please check this box. ___

131

DOCTORAL-GRANTING INSTITUTIONS THAT PROVIDED
USABLE DATA ON ACCEPTANCE RATES

Alfred University
Auburn University
Ball State University
Baylor University
Boston University
Brigham Young University
Brown University
Case Western Reserve University
Catholic University of America
City University of New York
Claremont Graduate School
Clarkson College of Technology
College of William and Mary
Colorado School of Mines
Colorado State University
Drexel University
Duke University
Emory University
Florida State University
Georgetown University
George Washington University
Harvard University
Indiana State University
Institute of Paper Chemistry
Iowa State University
Massachusetts Institute of
  Technology
Miami University
Michigan State University
Montana State University
Naval Postgraduate School
Newark College of Engineering
New Mexico Institute of Mining
  and Technology
New School for Social Research
Northeastern University
North Texas State University

Northwestern University
Occidental University
Ohio State University
Oklahoma State University
Pennsylvania State University
Polytechnic Institute of New York
Princeton University
Rutgers, the State University
South Dakota School of Mines
  and Technology
South Dakota State University
Southern Methodist University
Stanford University
SUNY (State University of New
  York), Binghamton
SUNY, College of Environmental
  Science and Forestry
SUNY, Stony Brook
Syracuse University
Texas Christian University
Tufts University
Union College and University
United States International University
University of Alabama
University of California, Irvine
University of California, San Diego
University of California, Santa Cruz
University of Connecticut
University of Dayton
University of Denver
University of Florida
University of Hawaii
University of Houston
University of Maine
University of Miami
University of Michigan
University of North Carolina
  at Chapel Hill

University of North Carolina
at Greensboro
University of North Dakota
University of Northern Colorado
University of Notre Dame
University of Oregon
University of Texas-Arlington
University of Texas at Austin

University of Vermont
Villanova University
Virginia Polytechnic Institute
and State University
Wake Forest University
Wayne State University
Wesleyan University
Yale University

TABLE D.1

Analysis of Institutional Response Rates by Quality of Institution

Roose–Andersen	Total Number of Graduate Schools in Category	Usable Responses	Percent of Total Population
4+	4	2	.5000
3.99 – 3.5	7	4	.5714
3.49 – 3.0	16	3	.1875
2.99 – 2.5	17	10	.5882
2.49 – 2.0	30	11	.3667
1.99 – 1.5	33	11	.3333
1.49 – 1.0	20	9	.4500
Less than 1.0	2	0	.0
Subtotal	129	50	.3876
Unranked	110	34	.3091
Total	239	84	.3515

TABLE D.2

Analysis of Institutional Response Rates by Number of Doctorates Awarded

Rank Size*	Total Number of Graduate Schools in Category	Usable Responses	Percent of Total Population
1 – 20	20	7	.3500
21 – 40	20	12	.6000
41 – 60	20	5	.2500
61 – 100	40	15	.3750
101 – 150	50	17	.3400
151 – 200	50	18	.3600
201 – 227	27	9	.3333
Subtotal	227	83	.3656
No Ph.D.'s in 1972	12	1	.0833
Total	239	84	.3515

*Graduate schools were ranked according to the total number of Ph.D.'s awarded in 1972.

TABLE D.3

Analysis of Institutional Response Rates by Region

Region	Total Number of Graduate Schools in Category	Usable Responses	Percent of Total Population
New England	24	11	.4583
Middle Atlantic	48	16	.3333
East North Central	36	12	.3333
West North Central	19	4	.2105
South Atlantic	31	14	.4516
East South Central	12	2	.1667
West South Central	24	9	.3750
Mountain	18	6	.3333
Pacific	27	10	.3704
Total	239	84	.3515

REFERENCES

Alchian, A., and A. Kessel. 1962. "Competition, Monopoly, and Pursuit of Money." Aspects of Labor Economics. Princeton: Princeton University Press.

American Psychological Association. 1972. Survey of Departments of Psychology, Spring 1972. Washington, D.C.

Astin, A. W. 1971. Predicting Academic Performance in College. New York: Free Press.

_____. 1975. Preventing Students from Dropping Out. San Francisco: Jossey-Bass.

Astin, H. S. 1969. The Woman Doctorate in America. New York: Russell Sage Foundation.

_____. "Career Profiles of Women Doctorates." In A. S. Rossi and A. Calderwood, eds., Academic Women on the Move. New York: Russell Sage Foundation.

_____, and A. E. Bayer. "Sex Discrimination in Academe. Educational Record 53: 101-18.

Attwood, C. L. 1972. Women in Fellowship and Training Programs. Washington, D.C.: Project on the Status and Education of Women, Association of American Colleges.

Bayer, A. E., and H. S. Astin. 1968. "Sex Differences in Academic Rank and Salary Among Science Doctorates in Teaching." Journal of Human Resources 111: 171-200.

_____. "Sex Differentials in the Academic Reward System." Science 188: 796-802.

Becker, G. S. 1957. The Economics of Discrimination. Chicago: University of Chicago Press.

Bem, S. L., and D. J. Bem. 1971. Training the Woman to Know Her Place: The Social Antecedents of Women in the World of Work. Department of Psychology, Stanford University.

Berelson, B. 1960. Graduate Education in the United States. New
    York: McGraw-Hill.

Bernard, J. 1964. Academic Women. University Park: Pennsylvania
    State University Press.

_____. 1965. "The Present Situation in the Academic World of Women
    Trained in Engineering." in J. A. Mattfield and C. G. Van Aken,
    eds., Women and the Scientific Professions. Cambridge, Mass.:
    MIT Press.

Breneman, D. W. 1970. An Economic Theory of Ph.D. Production:
    The Case at Berkeley. Berkeley: Office of the Vice President—
    Planning, University of California.

Campbell, J. 1970. "Change for Women—Glacial or Otherwise?"
    Women on Campus: 1970. A Symposium. Ann Arbor: Center for
    Continuing Education of Women, University of Michigan.

Caplow, T., and R. McGee. 1958. The Academic Marketplace. New
    York: Doubleday.

Carnegie Commission on Higher Education. 1973. Opportunities for
    Women in Higher Education: Their Current Participation, Pros-
    pects for the Future, and Recommendations for Action. New York:
    McGraw-Hill.

Cartter, A. M. 1966. An Assessment of Quality in Graduate Education.
    Washington, D.C.: American Council on Education.

Centra, J. A. Women, Men and the Doctorate. Princeton: Educational
    Testing Service, 1974.

Chalmers, E. L. 1972. "Achieving Equity for Women in Higher Educa-
    tion Graduate Enrollment and Faculty Status." Journal of Higher
    Education 43: 517-24.

Cohen, A., and A. Mesrop. 1972. "Women and Higher Education—
    Creating the Solutions." Washington, D.C.: American Psycho-
    logical Association, Task Force on the Status of Women.

Cross, K. P. 1972. "Women Want Equality in Higher Education."
    Research Reporter 8: 5-8.

_____. 1974. "The Woman Student." In W. T. Furness and A.
    Graham, eds., Women in Higher Education. Washington, D.C.:
    American Council on Education.

Davis, J. A. 1962. Stipends and Spouses: The Finances of American
    Arts and Science Graduate Students. Chicago: University of
    Chicago Press.

Department of Health, Education and Welfare. "Sex Discrimination"
    (DHEW Publication No. OCR 74-6). Washington, D.C.: DHEW.

El-Khawa, E. H., and A. Bisconti. 1974. Five and Ten Years after
    College Entry. Washington, D.C.: American Council on Educa-
    tion.

Epstein, C. F. 1970. Woman's Place: Options and Limits in Profes-
    sional Careers. Berkeley: University of California Press.

Feldman, S. D. 1974. Escape from the Doll's House: Women in
    Graduate and Professional School Education. New York: McGraw-
    Hill.

Fox, G. L. 1970. "The Woman Graduate Student in Sociology."
    Women on Campus: 1970—A Symposium. Ann Arbor: Center for
    Continuing Education of Women, University of Michigan.

Freeman, J. 1970. "Dissent." School Review 79: 115-18.

_____. 1972. How to Discriminate Against Women Without Really
    Trying. Department of Political Science, University of Chicago.

Freeman, R. B. 1973. "Decline of Labor Market Discrimination and
    Economic Analysis." American Economic Review 63: 280-86.

Graduate Record Examination Board. 1973. Graduate Programs and
    Admissions Manuals, vols. A-D. Princeton: Educational
    Testing Service.

Graham, P. A. 1970. "Women in Academe." Science 169: 1284-90.

Harmon, L. R. 1965. High School Ability Patterns: A Backward Look
    from the Doctorate. Washington, D.C.: Office of Scientific
    Personnel, National Research Council.

Harris, A. S. 1970. "Second Sex in Academe." AAUP Bulletin 56:
    283-95.

Harris, P. R. 1974. "Problems and Solutions in Achieving Equality
    for Women." In W. T. Furness and P. A. Graham, eds., Women
    in Higher Education. Washington, D.C.: American Council on
    Education.

Hole, J., and E. Levine. 1971. Rebirth of Feminism. New York:
     Quadrangle Books.

Holmstrom, E. I., and R. W. Holmstrom. 1974. "The Plight of the
     Woman Doctoral Student." American Educational Research
     Journal 11: 1-17.

Horner, M. "The Motive to Avoid Success and Changing Aspirations
     of College Women." Women on Campus: 1970. A Symposium.
     Ann Arbor: Center for Continuing Education of Women, Univer-
     sity of Michigan.

Husbands, S. A. 1972. "Women's Place in Higher Education. School
     Review 80: 261-74.

Jencks, C., and D. Riesman. 1969. The Academic Revolution. New
     York: Doubleday.

Kagan, J., and H. Moss. 1962. Birth to Maturity: A Study in Psycho-
     logical Development. New York: John Wiley.

Knapp, R. H., and J. J. Greenbaum. 1953. The Younger American
     Scholar: His Collegiate Origins. Chicago: University of
     Chicago Press.

Lewis, E. C. 1968. Developing Woman's Potential. Ames: Iowa State
     University.

_____. 1969. "Women in Graduate School." Graduate Comment 12:
     29-34.

Maccoby, E. E. 1966. Development of Sex Differences. Stanford:
     Stanford University Press.

Mitchell, S. B., and R. T. Alciatore. 1970. "Women Doctoral
     Recipients Evaluate Their Training." Educational Forum 34:
     533-39.

National Research Council. 1958-72. Summary Report on Doctorate
     Recipients in United States Universities. Washington, D.C.

Oltman, R. 1970. Campus 1970: Where Do Women Stand? Washing-
     ton, D.C.: American Association of University Women.

Parrish, J. B. 1962. "Women in Top Level Teaching and Research."
     Journal of American Association of University Women 55.

Patterson, M., and L. Sells. 1973. "Women Dropouts from Higher Education." In A. S. Rossi and A. Calderwood, eds., <u>Academic Women on the Move</u>. New York: Russell Sage Foundation.

Pifer, A. 1971. <u>Women in Higher Education</u>. Speech before the Southern Association of Colleges and Schools. Miami.

Radcliffe College. 1956. <u>Graduate Education for Women: The Radcliffe Ph.D.</u> Cambridge, Mass.: Harvard University Press.

Rees, M. 1974. "The Graduate Education of Women." In W. T. Furness and P. A. Graham, eds. <u>Women in Higher Education</u>. Washington, D.C.: American Council on Education.

Riesman, D. 1965. "Some Dilemmas of Women's Education." <u>Educational Record</u> 46: 424-34.

Roby, P. 1973. "Institutional Barriers to Women Students in Higher Education." In A. S. Rossi and A. Calderwood, eds., <u>Academic Women on the Move</u>. New York: Russell Sage Foundation.

Roose, K. D., and C. J. Andersen. 1970. <u>A Rating of Graduate Programs</u>. Washington, D.C.: American Council on Education.

Rossi, A. S. 1965. "Barriers to the Career Choice of Engineering, Medicine, or Science among American Women." In J. A. Mattfield and C. G. Van Aken, eds., <u>Women and the Scientific Professions</u>. Cambridge, Mass.: MIT Press.

_____. 1973. "Summary and Prospects." In A. S. Rossi and A. Calderwood, eds., <u>Academic Women on the Move</u>. New York: Russell Sage Foundation.

Rumbarger, M. L. 1973. "Internal Remedies for Sex Discrimination in Colleges and Universities." In A. S. Rossi and A. Calderwood, eds., <u>Academic Women on the Move</u>. New York: Russell Sage Foundation.

Sandler, B. 1972. <u>Health Services for Women: What Should the University Provide</u>? Washington, D.C.: Project on the Status and Education of Women, Association of American Colleges.

Scott, A. 1970. "The Half-Eaten Apple: A Look at Sex Discrimination in the University." <u>Reporter</u> (ERIC Document Reproduction Service No. ED 041 566).

Scott, A. 1973a. Preliminary Report on the Status of Graduate Women:
    University of California, Berkeley. Prepared for the Graduate
    Assembly's Committee on the Status of Women. Berkeley,
    March 30.

_____. 1973b. "Sex Differences in Graduate School Survival." Paper
    presented to the American Sociological Association, New York.

Siegel, A. E., and R. G. Carr. "Education of Women at Stanford Uni-
    versity." In Study of Education at Stanford 7. Stanford: Stanford
    University, 1969.

Simon, R., et al. 1967. "The Woman Ph.D.: A Recent Profile." Social
    Problems 15: 221-36.

Simpson, L. A. 1969. "Attitudes of Higher Education Employing Agents
    Toward Academic Women." Comment 12.

Solmon, L. C. 1973. "Women in Doctoral Education: Clues and Puzzles
    Regarding Institutional Discrimination." Research in Higher Edu-
    cation 1: 299-332.

Stark, R. 1967. Graduate Study at Berkeley: An Assessment of Attrition
    and Duration. Berkeley: Survey Research Center, Univerity of
    California.

Stiglitz, J. E. 1973. "Approaches to the Economics of Discrimination."
    American Economic Review 63: 287-95.

Theodore, A. 1971. The Professional Women. Cambridge, Mass.:
    Schenkman.

Tidball, M. E. 1973. "Perspective on Academic Women and Affirmative
    Action." Educational Record 54: 130-35.

University of Chicago. 1970. Women in the University of Chicago:
    Report of the Committee on University Women. Chicago.

U.S. Office of Education. 1971. Report on Higher Education.
    Washington, D.C.: U.S. Government Printing Office.

decision-makers, 11, 14, 36, 40, 41, 42, 63, 106 (see also, admissions)

Department of Health, Education, and Welfare (DHEW), 29

degree-completion, 6, 14, 15 (see also, time spent)

discrimination, 1-9, 23, 29, 34, 38, 56-57, 75; in admissions, 7, 38, 41, 42, 43, 46, 49-50; in financial aid, 83, 103; in faculty policies, 23, 33-35, 41, 105, 106; in legislation, 3, 35-37

dropout (see, attrition)

El-Khawas, E. H., 84

educational aspirations (see, aspirations)

employment, 22-24, 34-35, 40, 42, 60, 62-63, 72, 74 (see also, financial aid)

encouragement (see, counseling, motivation)

entrance requirements (see, admissions)

environments, 1, 7, 20, 31

Epstein, D. F., 9, 10

expectations (see, aspirations, socialization, stereotypes)

extracurricular programs, 61 (see also, interaction, faculty-student)

faculty, 1, 5, 41 (see also, interaction)

faculty, policies, 39, 40

faculty/student ratio, 32

family responsibilities, 15-17, 22, 30, 60-61, 72, 86, 106, 108

Feldman, S. D., 10, 12, 16, 21, 22, 24, 27, 29, 31, 36

fellowships, 16, 26-29, 89 (see also, financial aid)

field of study, 10, 13-16, 24, 28, 46, 60, 66, 67, 108

financial aid, 15- 16, 82, 108; as an obstacle to completion, 86, 89; assistantships as, 83-85, 93, 95; awarding of, 83, 89-93, 95, 101, 102, 103, 104, 107; differences by field of study, 15-16, 83, 92, 93, 95, 102, 103-104, 107; dollar value of, 84, 92, 93, 95, 96, 102, 103-104, 107; employment as, 15, 101; family or private support as, 27-28, 89, 92, 96, 101; fellowships as, 26-27, 85, 89, 92, 95, 96, 101; G.I. benefits as, 95, 101, 104, 107; government support as, 92, 93, 101; grants as, 83; impact of, 15, 16, 27-28, 83-85, 94, 107; information about, 28; and institutional characteristics, 101, 102, 103; institutional support as, 27, 86, 89, 93, 101, 104; loans as, 27, 28, 83, 89, 95, 96, 101, 104, 107; non-service awards as, 83, 95, 102, 103, 104; savings as, 27; service awards as, 83, 84, 95, 102, 104; spousal support as, 74; tuition waivers as, 95

financial need, 84-85, 86, 95-96, 103-104

Fox, G. L., 9, 19, 31

Freeman, J., 4, 7, 32

Freeman, R. B., 40

G.I. benefits, 95, 96, 104, 107

grades, 12, 13, 46, 106

Graduate Record Examination (GRE), 12, 46, 48, 50, 51, 52, 53, 54, 55, 72, 106 (see also, admissions, institutional quality)

Graduate Record Examination Board, 53

Graham, P. A., 19, 21

Greenbaum, J. J., 26

Harmon, L. R., 12, 24, 46

Harris, A. S., 5, 7, 11, 15, 16, 23, 25, 33

Harris, P. R., 8
health services, 1, 7, 35 (see also, counseling)
hiring, 36, 38, 40 (see also, faculty, policies)
humanities (see, field of study)
Hole, J., 12, 33
Holmstrom, E. I., 31
Holmstrom, R. W., 31
Horner, M., 9-10
humanities (see, field of study)
Husbands, S. A., 20, 32

institutional characteristics, 49, 50, 69, 71, 72, 74, 81, 82
institutional goals, 8, 23-24, 40-41
institutional policies, 1, 3-5, 9, 13, 29-31, 34-35, 50
institutional quality, 25-26, 29, 41-42, 43, 44, 45, 46, 48, 53, 54, 56, 57, 58, 64, 66, 67, 72, 106
institutional reputation, 22, 40-42
interaction, faculty/student, 19, 20, 31-32, 60-61, 84, 106
investment, education as, 6, 9

Jencks, C., 5, 8

Kagan, J., 9
Kessel, A., 39
Knapp, R. H., 26

labor market, 9, 42
legislation (see, affirmative action)
Levine, E., 12, 33
Lewis, E. C., 6, 9, 18, 30

McGee, R., 7, 8, 19
Maccoby, E. E., 9
major (see, field of study)
marital status, 15, 17-18, 27, 28, 61-63, 72, 81, 106 (see also, family responsibilities)

maternity leaves, 7
Mesrop, A., 28
Mitchell, S. B., 15, 17, 18, 22, 23
mobility, 17, 61, 75, 77, 81-82, 106
Moss, H., 9
motivation, 13, 14, 18-20, 60, 62, 108

National Center for Educational Statistics (NCES), 69, 75
National Institutes of Health (NIH), 75
National Research Council (NRC), 12, 24, 26, 64, 75
National Science Foundation (NSF), 13, 26
nepotism, 1

Oltman, R., 26, 30, 33, 35
opportunity costs, 15, 38

Parrish, J. B., 33
part-time (see, student characteristics, institutional policies)
Patterson, M., 15, 16, 17
persistence (see, attrition)
Pifer, A., 6, 37
placement, 60, 63
policy-makers, 37, 39
pregnancy (see institutional policies, maternity leave)
prejudice (see, discrimination)
prestige (see, institutional reputation)
productivity, 8, 22-25
professional school (see, field of study)
promotion (see, faculty, policies)
profit, 38, 39-40
publications (see, productivity)

quality (see, institutional quality)
quotas, 5, 13, 36

Radcliffe College, 22

recruitment, 34, 107, 108

Rees, M., 12, 15, 18, 19

recommendations, 13 (see also, assessment, of students)

research (see, field of study, institutional goals, productivity)

restrictions (see, barriers)

Riesman, D., 5-6, 8, 10, 20, 26

Roby, P., 4-5, 7, 9, 11, 12, 13, 14, 23, 27, 28, 29

role models, 32, 109

roles, 5, 8-10, 16, 21, 31 (see also, family responsibilities, socialization)

Roose, K. D., 40, 43

Roose-Anderson ratings (see, institutional quality)

Rossi, A. S., 10, 11, 35

Rombarger, M. L., 36

salary (see, faculty, policies; employment)

Sandler, B., 4, 35

Scott, A., 13

Sells, L. W., 10, 11, 14, 15, 16, 17, 18, 19, 31

selection (see, admissions, applicant pool, application rates)

Seven Sisters Colleges (see, women's colleges)

Sewell, W., 9

sex differences (see, discrimination, roles, socialization)

sex roles (see, roles, socialization)

Siegel, A. E., 17

Simon, R., 21, 22, 24, 26, 34

Simpson, L. A., 33

social mores (see, socialization, roles)

socialization, 2, 8-11, 17, 108

Solmon, L. C., 5, 14

sources of support (see, financial aid)

spouse (see, financial aid, marital status, roles)

Stark, R., 14, 15-16, 25, 28

Stiglitz, J. E., 40

Stereotypes, 4, 18, 60

Stipend (see, fellowships, financial aid)

stop out (see, attrition)

student characteristics, 49, 77; ability, 14, 32, 41, 42, 46, 72, 106, 107-108; age, 29, 30, 64; part-time, 22, 28, 29, 34, 35, 60; personality, 19-20, 32; self-image, 31

student/faculty ratio, 32

student/faculty relationships (see, interactions)

Theodore, A., 4

Tidball, M. E., 32

time spent, to earn degree, 15-18, 64, 66, 67-74, 106

tuition (see, institutional characteristics)

U.S. Office of Education, 5

women's colleges, 25, 32, 48

work (see, employment)

ABOUT THE AUTHOR

LEWIS C. SOLMON was born in Toronto, Canada, in 1942. He received his B.Com. from the University of Toronto in 1964, and his Ph.D. in Economics from the University of Chicago in 1968. Currently, he is Executive Officer of the Higher Education Research Institute in Los Angeles and Associate Professor in Residence at the Graduate School of Education, University of California at Los Angeles. He has taught at Purdue University, City University of New York, and Virginia Polytechnic Institute and State University, and been a Research Fellow and Research Associate at the National Bureau of Economic Research.

His books include Economics, Does College Matter? and Capital Formation by Expenditures on Formal Education, 1880 and 1890. He has published numerous articles in professional journals of economics and education, and served on a number of national advisory panels dealing with education-related issues.

THE CRISIS IN CAMPUS MANAGEMENT
George J. Mauer

MINORITY REPRESENTATION IN HIGHER EDUCATION
IN THE UNITED STATES
Frank Brown
Madelon D. Stent

THE WORLD'S STUDENTS IN THE UNITED STATES:
A Review and Evaluation of Research on
Foreign Students
edited by Seth Spaulding
Michael Flack